# PRAISE FOR
# THE 7 L's YOU MUST TAKE

"Superstar. That's what Erven Nelson's book can bring out in each of us. His personal story is as compelling as the content, insights, and inspiration he provides. I had heard of his quick career growth at Wawa and wanted to meet the person behind the story. I was immediately taken by Erven's charisma when we first met. It embodied positivity, kindness, and care, all of which you could tell were deep within his DNA. The learnings and life lessons in his book clearly stem from Erven's passion for helping others and are deeply influenced by the love and encouragement his mother provides as his role model. So, if you are looking to be inspired, seeking motivation, and want a plan to help you get to your own inner "Superstar," look no further. Erven is the real deal, and it's going to be fun watching him continue to grow his career, spreading positivity and influencing thousands of people along the way. He's inspired me; now it's your turn."

—Chris Gheysens, President & CEO, Wawa Inc.

"It has been my pleasure to know Erven Nelson for the last five years as Director of Operations, Florida Markets. The smile you see on the cover is the same smile Erven radiates every day and one I have come to love. Not only has he grown in his role at Wawa but as a son and role model of a human being. This book is unique because, unlike traditional authors, Erven did not have to research a topic to write on; he lived it, so these words are from the heart. The most important aspect of *The 7L's You Must Take*, which makes it practical but profound, is Erven's emphasis on building character rather than attaining success. There is no effectiveness without discipline and no discipline without character. When you engage with these pages, you will be engaging with Erven, the superstar released within."

—Steve Hasher, Region 10 Director of Operations, Wawa Inc.


"I remember when Erven was nine years old playing the piano, freestyle rapping, leading a youth group, and bringing an energy that screams confidence and much self-esteem. I knew Erven would succeed despite his many trials and unfortunate life circumstances. The 7L's are tried and true - you and your children will learn from an author that continues to release his "superstar" by these same lessons at such a young age. We're all in for a treat."

—Jemile Weeks, NY Mets Coach and founder of WeFam United Inc.


"During a winter evening in January of 2013, on my way home from an extremely long day of work, I stopped at a local fast-food restaurant to bring dinner to my family. It was already later than I had said I would be home, and I was at the end of a 14-hour day preparing my new store for its grand opening. Essentially exhausted, walking into the restaurant, I was greeted with a genuinely warm smile that immediately made me forget how tired I felt. His nametag read Erven, and the young man, simply put, had an unbelievable energy about him. It was infectious. The kitchen was backed up, and his coworkers were stressed, yet as he made his way throughout the workplace, he left each associate calm and refreshed. He kept me informed about my order and why it was delayed and offered some dessert for the extra wait. I declined the offer, but after observing him in action, I introduced myself, gave him my contact information, and asked him to hear me out about job opportunities. This began Erven's journey with Wawa and a relationship with myself, for I am forever grateful.

Having a front-row seat watching this man develop himself and persevere throughout his career has been motivating, inspirational, and humbling. Erven has taught me the power of having a positive attitude and the benefit of being gracious despite any perceived setbacks in life. Erven was very clear in his aspirations to be financially independent and his desire to give back to his community, but most of all, his desire to inspire others from similar backgrounds to see that success is achievable through believing in yourself and having attainable goals.

Erven has spent the past nine years creating and living *The 7L's You Must Take*. During this time, I have been fortunate to be a confidant, mentor, student, and friend of Erven. This journey has been some of the best moments of my career. He has now developed his method to succeed financially and mentally. This book is a straightforward step-by-step instruction to success for anyone who has felt stagnant, overlooked, devalued, and lost in their career. Please enjoy and utilize the book as Erven intended, as your book. By making this book your OWN, you will succeed and release the superstar within."

—Michael Carragher, Area Manager, Wawa, Inc.

# THE 7 L'S YOU MUST TAKE

To succeed financially and release the "superstar" within

Self-Help & Financial Literacy

## ERVEN NELSON

We want to hear from you. Please send your comments about this book to us at www.iamervennelson.com. Thank you.

Details in some anecdotes and stories have been changed to protect the identities of the persons involved.



*The 7 L's You Must Take Challenges*, is available at www.iamervennelson.com/challenges

Cover photograph of author: David Daudin

First printing, August 06, 2022

ISBN Number - Paperback: 979-8-9866482-0-0
ISBN Number - eBook: 979-8-9866482-1-7
Also available on audio at iamervennelson.com

Printed in the United States of America

PUBLISHER
Qloud 9 Publishing, LLC
Qloud9publishing@gmail.com

Author: Erven Nelson
For more information on the author, visit: www.iamervennelson.com

# AUTHOR'S NOTE

I designed this book to provide information that I believe to be accurate based on my personal experience. None of the content, opinions, and stories in this book should be interpreted as investment advice, individual needs, or other professional services such as legal or accounting advice. Seek the services of a professional if you need expert assistance in investment, legal, and accounting matters. This book represents my personal opinions and should be enjoyed as such. Please note that some people's names and identifying details in the text have been changed.

Don't passively *read* this book. Highlight sentences that stand out. Make it *your* book.

At the beginning of each lesson is a section called "Key Words" and "Objectives." There you will find:

- ❖ Key Words. These are words associated with the lesson.
- ❖ Objectives. This is what I want you to have learned or achieved by the end of the lesson.

In each lesson is a section called "Note to reader." There you will find:

- ❖ Note to reader. Key lessons and principles I want you to remember.

# CONTENTS

# THE 7 L'S YOU MUST TAKE

To succeed financially and release the "superstar" within

Self-Help & Financial Literacy

www.iamervennelson.com

# INTRODUCTION: MY STORY

When I was a kid, I watched my mother struggle and sacrifice a lot to raise our family, put food on the table, and make us feel special. Every Sunday night after church service, we'd have a family game night and play board games like Monopoly. The message was clear: quality family time was necessary. My mother deliberately made time for us, and we all made time for each other despite our busy schedules.

My mother was fifteen when she had my eldest brother, Tyreke. One year later, she had my sister, Shaniqua. Then she had my sister, Doris. By age eighteen, she had four children. My father died of a heart attack about two years after my birth. I never got to know him.

Imagine a young girl, barely in her twenties with only an eighth-grade education, trying to raise four kids on her own while recovering from the loss of her kids' father. My situation wasn't unusual; most of my friends in my community were fatherless. It was tough, but my mother did a great job raising us.

Fast forward to February 17, 1999: my mom was twenty-four with six kids. I remember watching her come home late at night from her second job exhausted. I remember my aunt Michelle frequently traveling from miles away to spend time with us and support us financially. Auntie Michelle never missed our birthdays or holidays. She knew how to make us feel loved despite our hardships.

My family often slept in shelters until my mother got approved for section 8 housing. While other kids dressed up in the latest fashions, we shopped at local thrift stores.

I remember my grandmother allowing us to move into her small two-bedroom apartment until my mother was financially stable. My grandmother slept in the main bedroom and my uncle occupied the second room. My siblings and I slept on the hard tile floors while my mom slept on a sofa in the living room. My grandmother loved us dearly. She just didn't have enough resources or square footage in her small apartment to comfortably shelter our family of seven.

We made the most of what we had. Antique decorations were attached to the eggshell-painted walls and an old television rested on a wooden stand inside the living room. My siblings and I rode two city buses to attend school in a higher-income area miles away. My mom didn't want us going to the school in our community. Of course, we had to use the home address of a friend who had more financial backing in order to get accepted into the school.

The more I watched my family struggle, the more determined I became to earn money. I aspired to purchase a house with acres of land big enough for my immediate family to live on. I wanted a white Range Rover instead of the purple Ford minivan that was my mother's treasure. I used to tell people I would be a Grammy award-winning music producer when I grew up. I loved creating music, and I believed someone would resonate with my story. I started playing piano and writing songs at twelve years old. Music was my platform to share my journey with the world. It was my escape.

My mother always referred to me as her "superstar" to remind me of my worth as a child. She always sees greatness within me and supports everything I do. Not only does she support my decisions, but she always makes me feel like I've made the right ones.

Despite my challenges and circumstances, I was promoted from Customer Service Associate to General Manager at Wawa, a Fortune 500 corporate retail company, and I opened four new locations in just over eight years. I received a reward for outstanding leadership. I graduated from high school and completed two years of technical school. I am passionate and committed to giving back. I founded the Seven Lessons Foundation to help future generations build character and wealth through mentoring and financial empowerment. I want to help them discover the "superstar" within.

My mother always shared valuable life lessons with my siblings and me. One that I remember to this day is, "Never give up no matter your circumstance. Always remember that you are my superstar." I did not understand what this meant as a child, but it all became clear as I got older.

My family, teachers, mentors, and the environments in which I grew up impacted my perspective of the world, and I will always be grateful for that. If I could go back in time, there are several lessons I would have loved to share with my mother. These are the seven lessons I believe will provide the tools, principles, and practices you must have and teach your children to succeed financially and release the "superstar" within.

Let me show you some photos of my life so you can get to know me.

Here's one of me and my mom when I graduated
from high school in 2013.

Here is me in my student-housing apartment doing what I love: producing music. I recorded three film soundtracks and multiple local artists out of that tiny home studio. I made the most of what I had at the time! Check out my latest work at iamervennelson.com/music.

# LESSON 1

## FIND YOURSELF

#understandtheassignment

*"You've got to follow your passion. You've got to figure out what you love and who you are. And have the courage to do that. I believe that the only courage anybody ever needs is the courage to follow your own dreams."*
*– Oprah Winfrey.*

# KEY WORDS

- ❖ Ego
- ❖ Character
- ❖ Integrity
- ❖ Brand
- ❖ Authenticity
- ❖ Fear
- ❖ Critical thinking

# INTRODUCTION

I did not write this lesson to fix you. I want you to shift your mindset into asking, "How can this lesson help me progress?" This lesson gives you the key insights and tools you can use to identify who you are meant to be.

# OBJECTIVES

When you have completed this lesson, you will have learned the following:

- ❖ Find yourself.
- ❖ Let go of fear.
- ❖ Protect your brand with integrity.
- ❖ Distinguish between Ego Left and Ego Right.

# FIND YOURSELF

The journey to finding yourself starts with internal transformation. It's about recognizing and strengthening your inward condition to perform as the best version of yourself. Think about a time when you experienced failure. What lessons did you learn? Let's be honest; it's challenging to take responsibility for what feels like your biggest failure. I have been there. I am not perfect, and I do not have all the answers.

To become the person I desired, I lost material things, entanglements, and even bad habits. Remember that you have value, and you are essential no matter your circumstances. The best version of yourself exists beyond your mental limitations.

Here is one principle to adopt for finding yourself:

**1. Ignore Social Norms and Accept Yourself and Your Path**: Unleashing your "superstar" within and embracing it will allow you to walk your purpose. This is what makes you unique. With today's social media, the internet, and technology, we are growing more disconnected from ourselves and our purpose.

To fill the gap between where you are now and where you want to be, you must ignore cultural and social pressures. I've met many people who live their lives conforming to social norms. Why? Because growing up, we have learned what to think, not how to think. Critical thinking is a manner of thinking beyond what someone tells you. Thinking that employs reasoning, self-reflection, analysis, open-mindedness, and curiosity. One way I apply critical thinking is by questioning what people tell me. I ask questions like, "how do you know this?"

When you apply critical thinking to your everyday life, you will begin to think more intentionally and make more impactful decisions. Most importantly, you will start to define your life. To practice ignoring social norms and accepting yourself, consider your social circle. Are you expected to act or dress a certain way? Avoid fitting into the definition of what the people in your social circle define as "acceptance." Start by creating a clear vision of how you see yourself and focus on that.

> **Note to reader: To fill the gap between where you are in your life and where you want to be, you must ignore cultural and social pressures.**

*"Indecision is a habit which usually begins in youth. The habit takes on permanency as the youth goes through graded school, high school, and even through college, without DEFINITENESS of purpose. The major weakness of all educational systems is that they neither teach nor encourage the habit of DEFINITE DECISION."*
*– Napoleon Hill.*

Identifying what brings meaning to your life gives you something to strive for each day. It gives you purpose. Some of us have nothing to look forward to outside of our jobs. Some live with no actual meaning in their lives. Your job, or lack of one, doesn't define who you are! Don't tie your self-worth to your profession. You could be the CEO of a corporation that makes millions of dollars but still be unhappy. Or you can be a cashier at a fast-food restaurant who changes others' lives with your kindness. The difference lies in how you approach life. Embrace who you are now and start acting like the person you want to become.

Negative opinions from others who intentionally hurt you for being different or standing out don't define you either. Some people find pleasure in bringing others down.

Do you feel this way when you're with your friends?

- ❖ Pressured to do things you don't want to do.
- ❖ Constantly gossiping about others.
- ❖ Put down with no care for your feelings.
- ❖ Not supported when you need them.

If you related to one or more of the points, consider reducing your association with them. Whoever told you that you weren't good enough or would never amount to anything was wrong. You will constantly be scrutinized by others no matter your position. They will always find something to say, but they don't know your journey, where you have been or where you are going, period. Whatever you want to do, believe in it more than anyone else. Whenever you have self-criticizing thoughts, speak affirmations and kindness to yourself.

Assess where you are in your life right now. All the pain, suffering, loss, and failure have contributed to who you are today. Instead of saying, "life isn't fair," I want you to turn your experiences into motivation and valuable lessons that will help you grow. One way to do this is by shifting your perception. You have the power to view your experience through a positive or negative lens. For example, you can take a difficult breakup and view it through a negative lens where you see yourself as the victim… or you can turn your experience into a positive opportunity to love yourself and continue to grow.

*"No such thing as a life that's better than yours."*
*– J-Cole, "Love Yourz"*

**Note to reader: Embrace who you are and start acting like the person you want to become.**

---

When I was a child, I remember my family living in a shelter until my mother was financially stable. Imagine a single mother raising six kids on her own, struggling to make ends meet. It was an extremely challenging stage for all of us, but she refused to quit. I know now that her children gave her life meaning, and she never gave up on us, no matter her circumstances. Today, I use that as motivation to always have the means to provide for myself. It instilled a sense of resiliency in me, and I use it to my advantage. I made a personal commitment that my family would never experience homelessness.

In the first box below, write what you find meaningful in your life.

<br><br><br><br><br><br><br><br><br><br><br>

In the second box above, write a series of short sentences that best describe why you find these things purposeful. Be specific.

Every time you make a choice, ask yourself, "Is this decision in line with my purpose?"

Review this challenge once a week for the next four weeks. Each week, assess where you are in your life at that moment.

> **Note to reader: When you apply critical thinking to your everyday life, you will begin to make more impactful decisions.**

*"Your work is going to fill a large part of your life, and the only way to be truly satisfied is to do what you believe is great work. And the only way to do great work is to love what you do. If you haven't found it yet, keep looking. Don't settle. As with all matters of the heart, you'll know when you find it. And, like any great relationship, it just gets better and better as the years roll on. So keep looking until you find it. Don't settle."*

*– Steve Jobs*

Some people are so concerned about their reputations that they sacrifice their core values and beliefs to be accepted in society. Don't focus on what people think about you. Taking this approach will contribute to losing yourself. You cannot expect to appease and cater to the opinions of everyone. No matter what stage of life you are in, you will reap incredible rewards when you commit to your purpose and concentrate on that.

> **Note to reader: No matter what stage of life you are in, commit to your purpose and concentrate on it.**

In 2013, my senior year in high school, I was a cashier in a fast-food restaurant. The job provided me with just enough money to support my mother with bills and buy the food I desired. However, it had no long-term benefits. I loved the customer service position because it put me in front of people, which was perfect for my personality. I was passionate about changing people's lives with my kindness each day.

Growing up, people characterized me as an extrovert. I was the class clown, and I got kicked out of class a few times for attempting to be the center of attention. I often performed songs in local and school talent shows that boosted my self-confidence. I'm the type of person who could walk into a room full of strangers and spark up conversations. People always told me I could light up a room with my presence alone. This personality and confidence helped me build authentic relationships with customers, making them want to continue shopping at the restaurant.

One evening, a customer I had never met before approached me for assistance. I provided an exceptional customer experience that led him to know more about me. After receiving his order, he asked to speak with me privately. He was a husky Caucasian guy wearing a simple polo, jeans, and tennis shoes. I assumed he was about to complain about something he had observed during his visit, but I was wrong. Instead, he shook my hand and introduced himself.

"My name is Michael Carragher, general manager at Wawa, a fast-growing convenience store in the Florida market," he said.

I had heard about Wawa on radio marketing campaigns, but I had never shopped there. He went on about how he admired my customer service, hustle, teamwork, and how I was following processes on the register and food-service area.

"We are planning to open many stores in this market, and someone with your personality, skills, and potential could go far with the company if you give us a shot," he explained.

He saw value in me and viewed me as a potential asset. I told him I would consider his offer, but I knew I had to conduct my own research first. We exchanged contacts and set a date for an interview.

The next day, I spoke to my supervisor about the new job opportunity.

"What? I can't lose you right now, kid. I can give you more money and even guarantee you full-time hours if that's what you want," he said.

A pay increase and guaranteed hours didn't sound like a bad idea for a kid one month away from graduating high school. The following workday, I received a pay increase. It was a surprise. I had worked with the company for over a year, and I had never seen a pay increase or promotion before.

Like most people, I fell into the trap of choosing more money over long-term success. I called Michael immediately and explained that I was grateful for the new opportunity, but I had to stay where I was because I needed the money to support my family. Of my five siblings, I was the only one with a job, and I was determined to help my mother.

Michael was very understanding. He respected me even more for being responsible and family-oriented. "Save my number because you will be calling me back soon," he said firmly.

"Why do you think that?"

"Any company willing to pay you more when you submit your resignation doesn't see the true value in you. Because if they did, you would've gotten that pay increase and guarantee of hours a long time ago. When you realize this for yourself, I will be one phone call away with the opportunity still on the table."

I thought long and hard about his words. I spent nights tossing and turning, contemplating if I had made the right decision. A few months later, I concluded that he was right. I graduated high school and realized I was stagnant in the corporate world. I had more money but no growth.

When I called Michael back to inquire about a job, he was eager to tell me that the opportunity was still available and that he would be honored to have me on his team at Wawa. I had called at the perfect time because he was opening a new store.

Michael opened a door that changed my entire life. A door that led to blessings and opportunities I could never have imagined. Later in the book, I'll elaborate more on the leadership roles I earned at Wawa. It all started with me being authentic and simply being myself. I put out positive energy in the universe and got positive results. Do the things that you genuinely want to pursue in life. Know your value and never let anyone, and I mean anyone, tell you what you can not accomplish.

> **Note to reader: Every time you make a choice, ask yourself, "Is this decision in line with my purpose?"**

# LET GO OF FEAR

*"Shoot for the moon. Even if you miss,*
*you'll land among the stars."*
*– Les Brown.*

There are many fears in this world, but we all have one roadblock that gets in the way of the goals we strive to accomplish. You will reach your highest potential when you let go of the fear of getting started or not being good enough. I challenge you to make choices fueled by positive intentions, not fear.

Of course,

*"Not every positive intention will have a positive result,*
*but it will be better than negative intentions."*
*– Zig Ziglar*

> **Note to reader: You will reach your highest potential when you let go of the fear of getting started or not being good enough.**

Some people avoid stressful situations because they are overwhelmed by fear. I will admit that some forms of fear keep us safe. For example, one of my dear female friends attained a concealed weapons permit because she feared walking the streets alone. If crime rates weren't rising in her neighborhood, then maybe she wouldn't feel so compelled to carry one.

My perspective has always been to cope with my fears by living a little. I didn't begin having this attitude until I went skydiving for the first time.

"You are crazy!" was all my co-workers could say.

"You are too young to risk your life skydiving," said a close friend.

My family couldn't believe that I would be interested in such a thrilling experience.

I heard a lot of mixed reactions, and sometimes I thought they might be right, but I didn't let that stop me. As the plane accelerated and rose into the atmosphere, my stomach clenched. My palms were sweating, and I felt like my heart had skipped a beat. The reactions I'd heard from co-workers, friends, and family lingered in my mind. Suddenly, all the precautions and directions previously mentioned by my instructor faded into the clouds.

"Are you ready?" asked my instructor, grinning from ear to ear.

I wasn't ready at all. As I sat on the edge of the aircraft and watched my feet dangle below, I asked God for forgiveness for everything I'd done that was unworthy. I closed my eyes, and just like that, I was soaring through the sky like a bird. The adrenaline that rushed through my body was something I had never experienced so intensely before. When I opened my eyes and observed how small the world was beneath me, I felt free. The fear disappeared. I was focused. As the parachute released and we began to descend, I was confident that I was safe.

Since then, I have approached my fears in real life with the confidence that everything will be all right. Sometimes you think about your ideas or goals too much when all you have to do is jump.

> **Note to reader: Sometimes you think about your ideas or goals too much when all you have to do is make the leap.**

For years, my childhood friend Dacoup worked as a commercial airline sales representative while raising Reign, his son. Frequently, he vented to me about how stressful his day had been and how he considered taking on a new career path in real estate. He made comments like, "It's stressful, exhausting, tiring, and repetitive." He was ambitious about finding a career field that he could be passionate about and enjoy doing each day. That's a characteristic I have always admired about him. He knew his worth, and he would never settle for anything less than what he felt he deserved. He demanded more pay and requested more time off to spend with his son, but he never got the results he was looking for without some conflict with management.

From my observation, he worked unhappily for the airline for so long because of job insecurity. He was comfortable with his pay, benefits, and stability. However, he felt like he wasn't living up to his full potential.

Being comfortable prevents you from growing and developing.

One day, Dacoup decided enough was enough. He got his real estate license and began his journey with 100% commitment, hustle, and focus. Today, I am proud to say that he closed a few deals and even purchased his own property. Not only is he earning more money, but he found the freedom and growth he desired.

*Perception*

*There are still pieces you can put together, as broken as you seem*
*As dark as it may be, there's a tiny light that can shine through*
*When life hits you hard, there's a window you can climb to*
*And when you do, you notice you've made it through*
*Through the lies, deceit, broken relationships, the failing dreams*
*Late-night cries, and no time to shut your eyes*
*So many moments you didn't realize*
*You survived.*
*by Straunje Austin*

# PROTECT YOUR BRAND WITH INTEGRITY

*"Your brand is your inner personality and outward identity."*
*– Erven Nelson.*

It is essential to build your business and brand with integrity. Integrity is the quality of being honest and having strong moral principles. Your brand is yourself, whether you are selling or not. Your presentation can play a huge role in your brand identity and can help you attract opportunities. People will form a perception of you everywhere you go. It is crucial to always present the best version of yourself. And that doesn't mean compromising your values or spending a fortune on the latest fashion. It means making the most of what you have and dressing appropriately for every occasion, even if it means waking up a few minutes early to iron your clothes before work, school, a date with your partner, or a meeting.

When I was a manager at a corporate retail company, part of my job responsibilities included ensuring that all my associates were completely in uniform.

One associate couldn't seem to get it right. Let's call him Carlos. Every day, his appearance was not to company standards. No matter how many times I coached him about the policy or sent him home, he didn't have enough passion to show up in full uniform.

I overheard him sharing his thoughts about me with another associate in the break room one day.

"I just feel like Erven takes his job way too seriously."

I had a private pep talk with him in my office. "What did you mean by the comment you made in the break room?"

He sat in silence for a moment. "I-I just feel like you could take it e-e-easy on me sometimes," he stuttered.

Carlos probably assumed I would respond aggressively because he had spread rumors about me to another associate. Instead, I did the total opposite. I smiled.

I understood how he had formed his perception. I wasn't the smartest or the most experienced, but I had more hustle and drive than any of my peers.

"I appreciate your honesty. But if you want to make the most out of your valuable time with this company, try taking it seriously," I suggested. "That's the type of attitude you must have every day to be successful. We implement the personal appearance policy because we're promoting a brand to the public. The uniforms create a professional appearance. It also sets a standard that customers expect to see."

I expressed that I didn't particularly like wearing slacks and a button-down to work every day. It wasn't my style. But I had to do what it took to make a professional impression on my boss and to stand out from my competition. I wanted corporate to know I was the best fit for my job. My peers perceived me as the guy who was always clean-cut and professionally dressed. I wanted the same for Carlos.

After hearing my perception, he seemed to relax a little. He thanked me for the advice and acknowledged that I had given him a whole new outlook on the importance of protecting his brand. Since then, I have not had an issue with his appearance.

Whether you are at work, a meeting, at school, or taking a trip to the grocery store, always consider how you could be perceived. There is no need to complain about it; create the reputation you want.

**Note to reader: Appear how you want to be perceived.**

I will never forget when I learned that having integrity could increase my success probability. I was about 21 years old when I had a conflict with my general manager. Let's call him Tom. He had worked many years for the company but had recently gotten transferred to my store. From day one, he made it very clear that everyone would have to prove themselves to him. Although he had a militant demeanor, I appreciated his solid business acumen. He didn't mind sharing his knowledge and expertise with anyone willing to grow. He had a good eye for identifying leaders, which led to the "big wigs" highly respecting his opinions. I wanted to be one of his selections for an upcoming promotion opportunity in the area, so I strived to work harder every day than everyone else.

One evening, when I was starting my shift, Tom confronted me about a concern from the previous morning. "Make sure you are following company policies and always doing the right thing," he demanded.

His approach completely caught me off guard. One of my core values is to do the right thing even when no one is around. "What do you mean?" I asked.

"I know you took an extended lunch break in the office yesterday," he replied.

The company provided paid breaks so that everyone could help out during peak hours. Employees were responsible for returning to work on time. If you extended your break time, you were held accountable for it. I had to take a 30-minute lunch break because I worked an eight-hour shift, and Tom had intoned that I had gone way over thirty minutes.

I was very aware of the policy, and I was positive that his assumption was wrong. I didn't have an issue accepting disciplinary actions for my mistakes, but first I had to be sure I had truly made a mistake.

"Would you mind showing me on camera where I allegedly extended my lunch break?" I asked.

"I already saw it on camera. The incident occurred around six o'clock in the morning." He smirked as if he knew he had caught me telling a lie.

Most employees would have avoided speaking up to their boss, even if they knew their boss was wrong, because they feared:

❖ Their boss wouldn't hear them.
❖ Taking a pay cut (if it was a conflict with hours).
❖ Loss of employment.

I had worked for the company for a few years and had established a trustworthy reputation, so I didn't fear any of those negative possibilities. Since we had downtime, I calmly asked if he could privately review the camera in the office with me.

"Sure," he replied.

I felt my anxiety build as we entered the office. We pulled up a chair as the door closed behind us and reviewed the camera. It was only a month ago when I had sat in that same chair, excited to learn new ways to increase the company's financials from Tom.

After reviewing the camera, there was a pause. Tom seemed startled when the camera didn't display what he'd said he observed. I was actually in the office for about fifteen minutes that day. I had cut my scheduled thirty-minute lunch break short because my team needed my support.

"I believe you mentioned you saw the incident on camera," I said, breaking the silence.

It was clear that Tom hadn't reviewed it. The camera footage exposed the truth. An employee had spread a false rumor, and Tom had believed it instead of valuing me enough to check the legitimacy of the story.

"I made a mistake," he replied.

Tom must have sensed how heated I was because he grabbed his lunch bag and other items and jetted out of the store to prevent the conflict from escalating. I didn't feel like Tom handled the situation professionally, and I didn't feel valued as an employee. I could've contacted the HR department or notified my area manager (his supervisor) about the conflict, but my compassionate side thought it wasn't the best move. So I decided to take a more challenging approach.

"How can I go to work every day having conflict with my general manager, who ultimately makes the decisions about my growth with the company and salary?" I asked myself.

I realized the issue was more extensive than Tom and I. We had a dysfunctional relationship, but I saw it as an opportunity to challenge myself to resolve the conflict without getting HR and the area manager involved. The promotion event was less than two months away, and I was determined to do what it took to get there. I would let nothing stop me from accomplishing my goal of being promoted to a supervisor. If I could resolve this conflict with my general manager, I would prove that I had what it took to be in a leadership role.

The next forty-five days were one of the most challenging periods of my career with the company. Tom and I lacked communication, trust, and teamwork. I arrived at work every day with a positive attitude, but internally I was raging. I thought about putting in my resignation multiple times, but I didn't allow my emotions to show. Customers wrote positive reviews about my customer service, other employees and managers enjoyed working with me, and I exceeded expectations in my job responsibilities.

**Note to reader: Reacting to a situation with anger leads only to regret, letting your "Ego Left" win. (We'll talk more about ego in the next section of the book.)**

Tom never attempted to make it right with me during that forty-five-day period. It's safe to say he let his "Ego Left" get the best of him. What he had shown me was that he didn't care. We may not have seen eye to eye, but I always respected and greeted him with a smile when we crossed shifts.

As we made it to the final day before the promotion event, the "Big Wigs" asked Tom to submit an email with the names of anyone he considered for the supervisor position. He called me into his office for a meeting. It was the first time he had planned a one-on-one meeting with me since the day of the incident. I assumed he would tell me I wasn't qualified for the supervisor position.

When I entered the office, Tom was sitting in his chair facing the computer with his back to me. My heart pounded and my body grew tense. I stood in front of the door as it closed behind me, too anxious to sit.

"I know our relationship wasn't the best over the last few weeks, but I would like to apologize for my behavior," he said, turning around. "If I was in your position and my manager treated me the way I treated you over the last few weeks, I probably would've resigned by now. I don't know what kept you motivated, but you have shown me so much about your character. It is undeniable that you're the best candidate for the supervisor position. I submitted your name for a promotion, and I do not doubt that you will be a great leader."

The wrinkles on my forehead vanished, and my body relaxed. I appreciated the opportunity, and I couldn't have been more proud of myself for how I'd handled the situation. I smiled, accepted his apology, and thanked him for selecting me. I got the promotion a few days later and transferred to a new store location. I will always be grateful for the lessons I learned from that experience.

If you ever come across a similar situation, remember to do the following:

1. Never lose sight of your goals, no matter how challenging your circumstances are.
2. Learn to forgive.
3. Protect your brand with integrity.

Use the following list of questions to help change your thinking before you leave your house each day:

1. Who am I when no one is looking?
2. What is my brand or reputation?
3. What two words do I want people to associate with me?
4. Am I living in appreciation and gratitude?
5. What makes me authentic?
6. Do I radiate love?

# DISTINGUISH BETWEEN EGO LEFT AND EGO RIGHT

What do you believe about yourself?

Your ego is your self-identity. It controls your thoughts, actions, and beliefs. Every experience you had from being a child until now has developed your ego.

Think of your life as a video game: you have the choice to choose between two characters, Ego Left and Ego Right.

Ego Left makes statements that give credit or place blame on oneself.

- ❖ Everything I accomplished is because of me.
- ❖ I am not good enough.
- ❖ I earned my wealth on my own.
- ❖ I will never be more than what I am.
- ❖ I took my company from the bottom to the top.
- ❖ I will never lose weight.
- ❖ I am a failure.
- ❖ My client would be nothing without me.
- ❖ I built my success.
- ❖ I am better than everybody.
- ❖ I am not worthy.

Ego Right believes everything in the universe serves a purpose and values failure as an opportunity for growth.

I've come to think of Ego Right like this:

- ❖ It embraces equality, diversity, and inclusion.
- ❖ It seeks opportunities to improve self and grow skills.

- ❖ It exercises positive thinking.
- ❖ It cultivates integrity.
- ❖ It puts others before itself.
- ❖ It is confident in its ability.
- ❖ It collaborates with others.
- ❖ It is resilient.
- ❖ It practices critical thinking.

When you create your character in a video game, you develop an unrealistic identity. You might make the body shape more physically fit because you're not happy with your own. You change the skin tone to a darker or lighter shade because you're not proud of who you are. Maybe you change the eye color or nose structure because you are unsatisfied with your facial features. That's your Ego Left. Ego Left is how you perceive yourself or desire to see yourself. Ego Right is the reality of yourself.

Ego Left is the animated character that thinks they are making the decisions while Ego Right is the one actually making the decisions. Imagine if your character in the video game felt that he or she was making it all happen without you pressing the buttons on the remote control. They would be just standing there inactive until *you* press the buttons. The reason Ego Left believes it is making the decisions is because Ego Right is making decisions based upon the perceptions or desires of Ego Left. This scenario is comparable to operating your life without actually executing a plan.

In conclusion, your perception of reality is *your* reality, but it may not be true reality. Let's keep it one-hundred; you are not defined by your environment, addictions, or past experiences. You must let go of the past and make decisions based on your future goals.

You may be asking, "How do I make a decision based upon reality and not my perception of reality?"

I suggest making decisions based on valid evidence and not on feelings. You choose how you want to live your life. Don't give anyone else the power to define it for you!

One of the oldest concepts of marketing, the rule of seven, says that a prospective buyer must hear an advertisement at least seven times before being "sold" on a product or service. Today, that number is much higher with social media and the internet. Subconsciously, you are advertising what you want for yourself.

Follow the steps below to recondition your mind and define your life.

**Step 1.** Choose the words to best describe the goal you want to accomplish. You must manifest what you want. Make sure the words you choose are definite. For example, you could say, "I am a doctor, a lawyer, a musician, a professional athlete, an educator, the CEO," or whatever goal you desire.

**Step 2.** Allot seven different times throughout a typical day that allows you to recite your affirmation. For example, as soon as you wake up and before going to bed at night. Other examples of times you can commit to your affirmation are when you use the restroom, at meals, brushing your teeth, and commuting to and from work.

**Step 3.** After 30 days, evaluate.

Here's the truth: reconditioning your mind to commit to a goal entirely is not an easy process. It is important to remember that following the steps above doesn't substitute hard work and focus. So don't go around telling your friends and family, "Erven said that if I claim who I am seven times a day for the next 30 days, I will mysteriously become whatever I want to be." Sorry to break it to you, but don't quit your day job yet. You still have to work harder than anyone else to achieve your goals in life. (We'll talk more about setting goals in the next lesson.)

> **Note to reader: You are not defined by your environment, addictions, or past experiences. Your mind will adapt to what you put in it.**

Some time ago, a co-worker came to me in desperation. Although he seemed to have had a great life (athlete, intelligent, fast car, attractive girlfriend), his home life was catastrophic. He felt as if he had hit rock bottom. As a freshman in college, he had worked a full-time job and lived with his parents who were going through a difficult divorce. He studied business but had harbored a passion for basketball since middle school.

A few days before the semester, he had found a room for rent near his college and job. The arguments and hostility between his parents and the stress from work had led to a challenging previous semester, so he was excited about getting his own space.

The night before he planned to move out, he packed everything he owned into his car: his rental space expense, clothes, and shoes. He stopped at a neighborhood gym the following day to play basketball, which was part of his daily routine. Unfortunately, after running a game or two, he noticed his car was missing from the parking lot. He had lost everything: his car, wallet, clothes, shoes, and other personal items. In his wallet were fees for the upcoming semester, payments for the rental space, and his license.

You can probably assume that he moved back in with his disconnected parents and couldn't start taking classes until the following semester. His job was in jeopardy because he no longer had reliable transportation to work. He felt others were responsible for his unhappiness.

One day, he asked me for advice. I told him to shift his negative thinking into gratitude. I encouraged him not to give up and helped him discover the "superstar" within.

A month later, a police officer found his stolen Honda abandoned in a dark alley. It appeared that someone had been racing in the car because the tires were burned out, which was an inexpensive repair. He got his car back and landed a job opportunity that offered more money and better benefits. The following semester, he went back to college and continued down his career path. He said to me, "I did everything you said, and I already see different results."

He took ownership of his life during this process. He learned that he may have lost material items and experienced a setback, but it was not the end of the road, and he did not lose everything.

You lose everything when you give up on yourself.

---

**Note to reader: Negative outcomes are not the end of the road. You lose only when you give up on yourself.**

# EGO ACTIVITY

**Rules:**

You have 25 tokens allotted to describe who you are as a character. The number of tokens is less than the number of choices you have to make. Although you may think you possess all of the qualities below, 25 tokens will help you identify which attributes you believe are more important than others.

**Purpose:**

This challenge is designed to increase your self-awareness and identify your ego positively.

**Directions:**

1. Bubble in the spaces next to each quality to represent what you think of yourself. (As best as you currently see yourself.) You must use all 25 tokens.

Attractive         ◯ ◯ ◯

Intelligent        ◯ ◯ ◯

Committed          ◯ ◯ ◯

Loyal              ◯ ◯ ◯

Funny              ◯ ◯ ◯

Motivated          ◯ ◯ ◯

Healthy            ◯ ◯ ◯

Charitable         ◯ ◯ ◯

Confident          ◯ ◯ ◯

Positive           ◯ ◯ ◯

2. Take the same 25 tokens. In this step, bubble in the spaces next to each quality to represent how others see you. You must use all 25 tokens.

Attractive      ◯◯◯

Intelligent     ◯◯◯

Committed       ◯◯◯

Loyal           ◯◯◯

Funny           ◯◯◯

Motivated       ◯◯◯

Healthy         ◯◯◯

Charitable      ◯◯◯

Confident       ◯◯◯

Positive        ◯◯◯

**Note:** All of the qualities listed above are positive. You may have rated yourself higher in one attribute than the other, which is okay because a person who sees themselves in a positive light will perform better. When you accurately know yourself, you will make decisions based on an honest perception of who you are. Ask yourself, "Am I making decisions based on how the world sees me or how I view myself?"

Pause and take the time to seriously consider what you have just read. Don't rush to the next lesson without reflecting on what you have learned.

# LESSON 2

## SET ATTAINABLE GOALS

*"Motivation is like drinking a double espresso: it gets you going for a while, but eventually, you'll crash. The key is staying motivated by setting attainable goals that will help you stay focused until you reach your desired results."*
*– Erven Nelson*

# KEY WORDS

- ❖ Goals
- ❖ Motivation
- ❖ VALUE System
- ❖ Plan
- ❖ Strengths
- ❖ Weaknesses
- ❖ Leader
- ❖ Title

# INTRODUCTION

The purpose of this lesson is to help you create efficient goals and plan to execute them.

# OBJECTIVES

When you have completed this lesson, you will have learned the following:

- ❖ Motivation is temporary.
- ❖ How to stay motivated and focused.
- ❖ VALUE system.

# MOTIVATION IS TEMPORARY

Motivation is like drinking a double espresso: it gets you going for a while, but you'll crash eventually. When you feel motivated, suddenly you feel as if you can reach the results you desire instantaneously. How often has a motivational speech gotten you excited about going after your aspirations, only for you to be back to your old habits shortly after? The key is having the discipline to stay motivated and focused until you reach your desired results.

Before you can achieve your goals, you must have a plan. That plan is your step-by-step process of small, achievable goals. Goals give you direction, and the plan keeps you focused. I created the VALUE system to help you develop efficient goals and a plan to execute them.

**VALUE System**: the process of creating efficient goals and the plan to execute them. If you are willing to try this technique, read the insights and information below. Implement it in your life daily.

- ❖ Vision
- ❖ Actions
- ❖ Loyalty
- ❖ Unity
- ❖ Evaluate

# VISION

*"It's only a dream until you write it down,*
*and then it becomes a goal."*
*– Emmitt Smith.*

The first step to setting goals is to have a vision.

Create a mental image of what you want to happen. Once you have a clear picture of your goal, write it down. It is important to remember that you must align your vision with your goal. Think about your vision when you encounter a setback on your journey.

Imagine a pilot flying a plane with no destination. Now imagine if you were a passenger on that plane. You would go wherever the pilot takes you, hoping they find a safe place to land before the plane runs out of fuel. This scenario is comparable to you living your life without a vision. You must see the destination before you arrive. Ask yourself, "Am I the pilot or the passenger?" Don't let corporate America, family, friends, or irrelevant trolls on social media decide what you will be. Visualize your destination and take action to get there.

> **Note to reader: You must see the destination before you arrive.**

I'm writing this section of the book at a local bookstore. I chose to write in this environment because it inspired me to finish the book. Of course, I pick up a book and read it from time to time. I even purchased a few. I'm writing or observing the hundreds of consumers that shop at this location most of the time. Anyone who picks up a book written in the same category as mine, I ask them why they picked that particular book over thousands of other competitors. I'm capitalizing on the opportunity to soak in all the honest feedback I could gain.

"Is the author interesting or relatable to them? Is it the cover design that caught their eye? Was it word of mouth that drew interest? What is pushing them over the buying edge?" I'd ask myself.

One of my goals is to get my book on the shelves and displays of major book distributers. I can see my prospective audience sitting in the lobby or café reading my book. You must put yourself in environments aligned with your goals. Doing this will reinforce your passion and encourage you to keep going. I'm not the most competent or most experienced writer out there, but I'm determined to do what it takes to get this book in your hands.

Having a vision will put you 20% closer to accomplishing your goal.

---

**Note to reader: Once you have a clear picture of your goal, write it down.**

# ACTIONS

*"To me, ideas are worth nothing unless executed. They are*
*just a multiplier. Execution is worth millions."*
*– Steve Jobs.*

Draw up and execute a plan to reach your desired goal. Be sure to organize timeframes to get stuff done in your plan. It doesn't have to be complicated—just something you can easily understand.

Execution is the key to success. One way to execute your goal is by breaking it into smaller, achievable goals. For example, when I try to clean my kitchen, I divide the area into three sections and work on one section at a time. I start with the dishes. Then I wipe down the counters and equipment. Lastly, I sweep and mop the floors. This process ensures progress with no procrastination.

Decide on a date to update the progress of your goals. Due to economic reasons or market changes, you may have to change the deadline or rewrite the plan entirely.

Drawing up and executing a plan puts you 40% closer to accomplishing your goal.

# LOYALTY

*"Desire is the key to motivation, but it's determination and commitment to an unrelenting pursuit of your goal – a commitment to excellence – that will enable you to attain the success you seek."*
*– Mario Andretti.*

On the lines below, sign your signature to fully commit to the plan you created in the previous step. Your commitment will help you overcome the obstacles on your journey to accomplishing your goal and any other potential resistance to change. You are committing to executing your plan, no matter what!

_____________________________

_____________________________

If you want to become a professional athlete, you are the one who has to put in the training. If your goal is to become a lawyer or a doctor, you are the one who has to commit to years of studying. If you are working in corporate America, you are the one who has to stay late at work to finish your tasks, pick up shifts, and take on more job responsibilities to become the role you desire.

Committing to your plan puts you 60% closer to achieving your goal.

*"It's only crazy until it happens."*
*– Michael Todd.*

# UNITY

*"Talent wins games, but teamwork and*
*intelligence win championships."*
*– Michael Jordan.*

Identify the team of people you need to collaborate with to get closer to accomplishing your goal. Write their names on a sheet of lined paper.

In the boxes below, identify your strengths and weaknesses. Strengths are things you can use to push yourself forward. Weaknesses are areas you need to improve on.

**STRENGTHS**

**WEAKNESSES**

Consider bringing someone else to your team whose strengths align with your weaknesses to help you succeed.

Once you have identified the people you need to collaborate with and established your team, the key is to gain commitment and buy-in from them to your vision. Imagine if a single employee tried to operate a Wawa corporation alone. How successful do you think they would be? It's physically impossible for one individual to manage hundreds of Wawa locations. Something like this takes a broad network of internal and external partners who support the vision.

Identifying the team of people you need to collaborate with to accomplish your goals puts you 80% closer to achieving your goal.

> **Note to reader: The key is gaining commitment and buy-in from your team to your plan and goals.**

# EVALUATE YOUR PLAN

*"By failing to prepare, you are preparing to fail."*
*– Benjamin Franklin*

Take out a sheet of lined paper. Write any progress you made toward your goal. (It can be the number of tasks done or what you accomplished up to the date you committed to.)

Review your plan and be open to making changes. It will provide some accountability and allow you to grow.

The evaluation period will give you a better understanding of your mistakes and help you consider possible paths for improvement. During this process, consistently communicate results to your team and celebrate the little wins until you meet your goal.

When the goal is complete, you will reach the 100% mark.

When you have implemented the VALUE System in your life, I'd like to hear from you. Please reach out to me on Instagram or Twitter @iamervennelson or visit www.iamervennelson.com.

> **Note to reader: When you realize you are comfortable where you are, observe opportunities that make you uncomfortable to expand your horizon.**

---

People often feel burned out and frustrated in their careers because they've stagnated. It's so important to have something concrete to work toward.

Wawa was a rapidly expanding company in the Region 10 Florida market, and I wanted to seize every opportunity to grow. As a customer service associate, I set a long-term career goal to be a general manager, seven titles away from my position, and to train and develop other leaders. It seemed so far-fetched for a nineteen-year-old kid, but I was determined to do whatever it took to get there. Although I wasn't making a lot of money, I knew it wouldn't compare to what I would earn long term as a general manager with the right plan.

Pay vs. culture is a common debate in the workforce. You can work for a company that pays well but has an unhealthy culture. Or you can work for a company with an exceptionally healthy culture but unappealing pay. I chose Wawa because it had the right culture. A culture that represented diversity, inclusion, and equality. I evaluated long-term benefits that could improve my life. I focused on my 401k company match, employer stock ownership plan, skill-building, and career growth.

Using the VALUE system, I set a long-term goal to become a general manager. My small attainable goals were the seven promotions it would take to get there. Moving from team to team has been a rewarding experience. I've gotten the opportunity to train and develop others, broaden my skill set, and gain lots of relevant experience. I became a better leader.

Accomplishing my long-term goal of becoming a general manager at twenty-seven years old was fulfilling. I had finally gotten the title I desired. It was my golden ticket to the life my wife and I wanted. I knew that if I secured the title, I would always be in a position to financially provide for my family.

Titles do not make you a leader, and they do not define who you are. However, it does give you leverage. Leverage to continue growing in the work you enjoy doing with the compensation you desire. For example, if you are well paid by your current employer, you could negotiate a higher salary with the next employer.

The income was high, but there was a lot of responsibility that came with it. Whatever the challenge, I demonstrated my resilience to make corporate notice me.

> **Note to reader:** A leader is someone who puts others first. A leader takes responsibility and accountability for their actions. One key to becoming a successful leader at work is knowing the expectations, setting small attainable goals, communicating your plan with your team, being willing to get better, gaining commitment and buy-in from your team, celebrating small accomplishments, and consistently sharing results.

## MY INTERNAL PROMOTIONS:

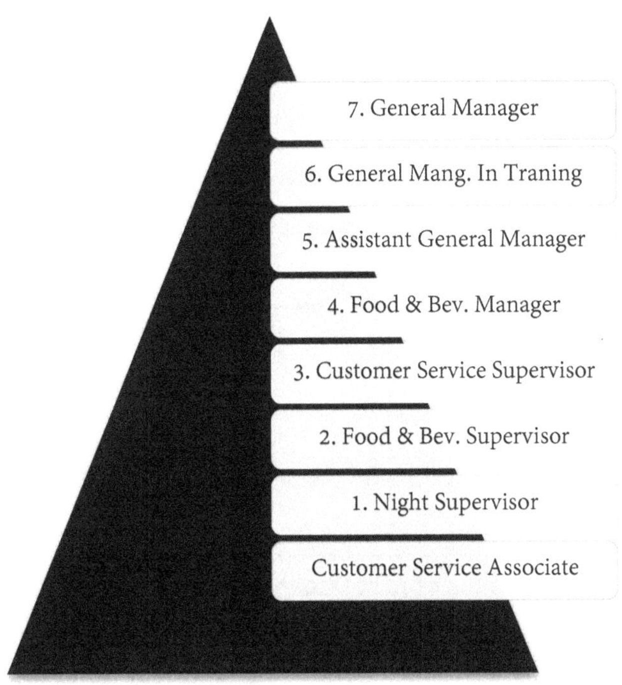


The road to my success hasn't been smooth. At the beginning, I didn't have any management experience or business education. I measured myself against people who were where I wanted to be, like Carragher, who was eventually promoted to an area manager position. I earned my first two promotions while juggling being a freshman in college and embracing new "adulthood" responsibilities. My expenses became my responsibility. I worked holidays, weekends, vacations, and I put in long hours and took on more significant projects.

Becoming a general manager was a pivotal moment in my career. I experienced many challenges, but I didn't let that stop me. The education and experience I gained from my mentors and my upbringing and experience had a powerful impact on my growth.

However, after I accomplished my long-term goal, I realized it wasn't the end of the road. I focused on the next promotion, pay increase, and the next chapter in life. The lesson I learned through the experience was never to stop setting new goals. Once you reach the finish line, dream bigger and set a new goal to reach an even higher level of growth and success.

> **Note to reader: Measure yourself against people who are where you want to be.**

> **Note to reader: You control how your peers perceive you. Be the person who seeks opportunities to continually improve your skills and develop others to be the best version of themselves.**

Pause and take the time to seriously consider what you have just read. Don't rush to the next lesson without reflecting on what you have learned.

# LESSON 3

## STRESS IS TEMPORARY

*"Leaders spend 5% of their time on the problem & 95% of their time on the solution. Get over it & crush it!"*
*– Tony Robbins.*

## KEY WORDS

- ❖ Stress
- ❖ Good Stress
- ❖ Bad Stress
- ❖ Three P's Method

# INTRODUCTION

The purpose of this lesson is to help you minimize or avoid some of the stress in your life.

> **Note to reader:** There are many different types of stress. In this lesson, I will refer to acute stress. Webster's dictionary defines acute stress as intensifying conditions leading to a culmination or breaking point. If you are experiencing chronic stress or you find yourself unable to cope with everyday life, please consult with a professional.

# OBJECTIVES

When you have completed this lesson, you will have learned the following:

- ❖ Perceived negatively vs. actual negative stressors
- ❖ The Three P's Method
- ❖ Good stress vs. bad stress

# PERCEIVED NEGATIVELY VS. ACTUAL NEGATIVE STRESSORS

Stress can come from anywhere. Webster's dictionary defines stress as a state of mental or emotional strain or tension resulting from adverse or very demanding circumstances. School, trouble at work, unhappy relationships, financial problems, and family can all be a source of stress.

In most cases, you feel stressed because your perspective cannot generate an answer to how you will get through a seemingly challenging circumstance. Your mind cannot determine the difference between perceived negative and actual negative stressors. For example, let's say you are lying in bed thinking about an adverse event so much that you can feel the emotional stress of it. As a result, your body reacts the same way as if you were there.

Your journey to success will be long and exhausting. It will also be challenging and demanding. It's okay to fail and cry out sometimes, but don't feel defeated. Once you release that emotional energy, face your obstacles with a positive attitude and figure out how you will overcome your circumstances. Worrying doesn't add happiness or more time to your life. Don't focus on the situation; take ownership and seek solutions to get out of the problem.

> **Note to reader: Don't focus on the situation; take ownership and seek solutions to get out of the problem.**

# THE THREE P'S METHOD

Stress can lead to health conditions like depression, anxiety, and high blood pressure. I've created The Three P's Method to help you minimize or avoid some of the stress in your life. I have used this method time after time; it is how I survive overwhelming circumstances. If you are ready to test this technique, read the steps below.

**Step 1.** Plot. Take deep breaths in and out until you feel released internally. Dwelling on the problem at hand won't make your life any better. Instead, identify what caused you to feel stressed, and create a plan for how you will get out of your situation. This process can be incredibly challenging, but you can do it!

**Step 2.** Positive Thinking. Challenge yourself to view the perceived stressful circumstance with a positive eye. Think of one experience in your life that made you feel exceptionally grateful. It could be big or small. The purpose of this step is for you to subtitle negative thoughts with gratitude.

**Step 3.** Perseverance. Stress is temporary. Once you know that what you are stressing about is perceived negative and not an actual negative stressor, you will probably agree that stress is temporary. If your experience is an actual negative stressor, your body/mind will return to its natural state without lasting negative effects after following the previously mentioned steps. So don't give up too soon because you won't allow yourself to get through it.

## GOOD STRESS VS. BAD STRESS

Often, when we talk about stress, we perceive it negatively and do not look at the benefits of having good stress. Good stress is needed to add excitement to your life. It's the type of stress that doesn't involve a threat or fear. Examples of good stress include buying a home, receiving a promotion, or getting married. You may also experience good stress while utilizing the VALUE System (as mentioned in Lesson 2).

Imagine you are getting on a roller coaster. You feel a rush of adrenaline, which contributes to good stress. You might feel nervous, but you are so thrilled about the experience that it stimulates you. It's an emotional challenge, but somehow you feel in control, and your mind senses that everything will be all right in the end. Now let's compare the same scenario to someone who may have had a horrendous experience on a roller coaster. This experience will contribute to bad stress because the perception of the experience negatively affects their mind, making them feel fearful or even threatened. What may be good stress to you may not be good stress to others. Ask yourself, "Is my situation perceived as threatening, or is it life-threatening?"

# PROPOSAL DAY

Although I am divorced, let me take you through my proposal day. A few weeks before I planned to propose to my best friend, whom I'd been dating for a little more than a year, I wanted to ask her father for his blessing. One day, while her father and I were alone in his home, I detected an opportunity to take my shot at creating one of the most extraordinary moments of my life. I asked for his blessing.

Before he could say a word, he embraced me with a hug. "I already feel like you are my son," he said. He cried tears of joy before genuinely saying yes, and my anxiety instantly disappeared.

A few days later, I wanted to involve her mom in the joyous proposal, so I had her help me select the perfect ring. She was elated at the idea, and she expressed that she couldn't have felt more honored to be part of the experience.

On December 27, 2019, proposal day, the plan was to convince my partner that we would spend the weekend at my parents' house, three hours away from ours, but we were actually meeting at her parents' house in town for the proposal. Shockingly, it worked.

I wanted to ensure that her nails looked the best possible before she tried to share up-close photos of her ring with friends, family, or on social media. So I had scheduled her a pedicure and manicure appointment a few days earlier. As we packed our bags and headed out for the trip, I told her we needed to stop at her parents' house to pick up equipment for my mom. I needed a reason for us to get to the proposal event.

We dressed in elegant attire because my mom had invited us to dinner at a restaurant.

Her parents lived about thirty minutes away from our house. Thankfully, they did all the decorations and food preparation before we arrived, so all I had to do was deliver the bride-to-be.

When we entered her parents' house, the dimmed lights and slow R&B music playing from the speaker at a low volume set an intimate tone. As we walked up the stairs toward the living room, she saw both of our parents, immediate family, close friends, and her co-workers on the far right side.

"What's going on?" she asked. She had her hand over her mouth to hide her shock, but I could see from her eyes that she was smiling.

To the left, pictures of us hung from the ceiling by string, ocean scented candles breezed in the atmosphere, and rose petals were arranged on the floor in the shape of a heart. A sign read, "MARRY ME."

Everything was perfect.

I pulled myself together, held her hand, and led her to the area where I would propose. I was filled with anxiety and perceived bad stress.

When she said yes, my anxiety and stress faded away. The perceived bad stress I had been experiencing throughout the process was actually good stress.

> Pause and take the time to seriously consider what you have just read. Don't rush to the next lesson without reflecting on what you have learned.

# LESSON 4

## SEIZE THE OPPORTUNITY

*"Instead of complaining, seize every opportunity, small
or large, through all steps in your career path."*
*– Erven Nelson*

*"Imagine being on your death bed, and standing around you is the ghost
of the dreams, the ideas, the abilities, and the talents given to you by
life… That, for whatever reason, you never went after that dream. You
never acted on those ideas. You never used those talents. You never used
those gifts, and there they are, standing beside your bed, looking at YOU
with large, angry eyes saying we came to you and only you could have
given us life! And now we must die with you forever."*
*– Les Brown*

## KEY WORDS

- ❖ 401 (K) Company Match
- ❖ Employer Stock
- ❖ Tuition Reimbursement

## INTRODUCTION

The purpose of this lesson is to help you seize the most out of every opportunity, small or large, through all steps in your career path.

## OBJECTIVES

When you have completed this lesson, you will have learned the following:

1.  How to seize the opportunity.

# SEIZE THE OPPORTUNITY

*"When you change the way you look at something,*
*what you look at will change."*
*– Wayne Dyer.*

At first, working in corporate America was stressful and time-consuming. I dedicated years to making someone else's family rich instead of my own. I didn't know how to make my hard-earned money make more money. I gave a vast portion of my earnings back to the government and lived off what remained. For years, I repeated this process. I felt blocked from moving toward my true purpose, and I relied on someone else to grant me a promotion or pay raise.

Here is how it works:

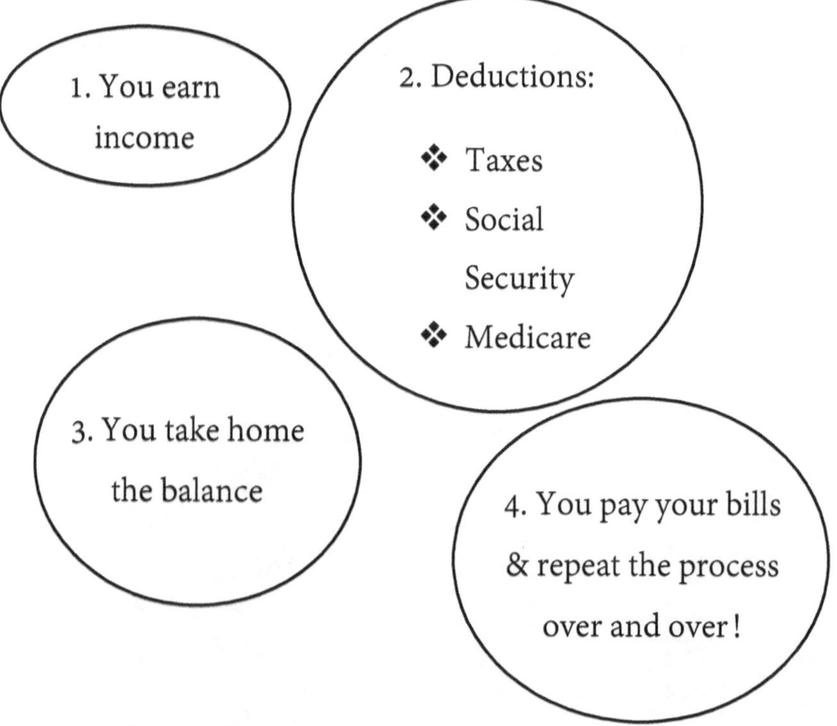

Over the years, I learned that positive thinking could change my work life. Once I developed confidence in myself and designed a plan for my life, all the frustration and annoying people didn't bother me as much. I've learned that you perform at your highest potential when working with purpose; having this mindset is when the work becomes easy.

It was not corporate America's fault that I was miserable. I blamed myself for giving someone else the power to control my destiny.

Chances are, you hate your job because it doesn't do enough for you. The solution is to make it work for you. I'm not saying work for someone else until retirement. All I'm saying is tap into every benefit that could apply to you. Make the most out of what you have until you get where you want to be (and while you're there, be excellent.)

> **Note to reader: You perform at your highest potential when you work with purpose; this mindset is when the work becomes easy.**

Here are a few solutions to change your narrative at work:

## 401(K) COMPANY MATCH

A 401(K) is a retirement plan that employees can contribute to. Employers may also make matching contributions. Find out if your job offers 401(K) benefits. It is to your advantage to match the maximum amount your employer is willing to contribute. Remember, a 401(K) plan is not liquid, so it's not easy to access. However, you can take advantage of the funds if you have a concrete plan.

A few hardship distributions your plan may include are repair costs for damages to your principal residence, costs related to avoiding foreclosure or eviction, purchase costs for your principal home, tuition, and medical expenses. Consult with a professional to get the information tailored to your specific 401 (K) plan.

I know what you're thinking:

"I can barely afford to pay my bills, so why would I deduct additional money from my pay into a 401(K) plan?"

Say you have a jar, and I told you that if you put in $5, I would match you with $5. But what if I said I would give you $10 if you put in $10? If you had the option to choose both, which one would you choose?

In 2014, I learned that my employer offered 401(k) employee match benefits up to 5% of my pay. I decided to put in 5% to get the most out of it. When my apartment management team raised the monthly rent, I was devastated. I tried so hard to figure out how to make it work until I could level up and dream higher. I needed a solid financial plan to acquire a home while still sustaining a decent lifestyle, so I spoke to a local mortgage company and got approved for an FHA loan that required a 3.5% down payment of the purchase cost.

Exploring my options, my plan advisor informed me I would not be penalized if I took out a 401(k) loan for a principal residence purchase cost. In December 2020, during the COVID-19 pandemic and an extremely competitive market, I knew it was the right time to invest while rates were low. I borrowed funds from my 401(k) to cover the down payment and closing cost of a property I was interested in and used my liquid cash for minor renovations and furniture. I took advantage of the opportunity and made it work for me.

Some would say I made a mistake in borrowing money from my retirement savings. Dave Ramsey, someone I admire, would probably disagree with my decision. I assessed the risks and rewards before I made my move. Even if I lost, I figured I would still come out with something valuable—real property. My long-term plan was to accumulate equity on the property to build long-term wealth. Eventually, I would be able to convert the property into a rental and get a monthly return on my investment. I'm not suggesting that this is the best approach for your situation. I'm just pointing out what I did to make my money work.

# EMPLOYER STOCK OWNERSHIP PLAN

Some employers offer employee stock purchase plans so associates can purchase shares of company stock. If your company offers employee stock purchase plans, find out how long the vesting period is. Vested shares are shares you own even if you get fired or quit.

For example, Rebecca worked for a company that offered employee stock purchase plans. Associates could not purchase stock shares, but the company contributed to the vested account yearly. They required a six-year vesting period before an associate could own 100% of their shares. Rebecca worked at the company for several years and earned over $30,000 in her account. She quit her job and invested the money into a four-bedroom property. She lived in one room and listed the other three rooms for rent. The money that came in from the rentals provided a high passive income.

# TUITION REIMBURSEMENT

Some employers offer tuition reimbursement to help further their employees' education and training. If you are in college or looking to start and your job offers tuition reimbursement, it is to your benefit to work there until they pay off your tuition.

Jessica, a former associate, worked for a corporation that offered tuition reimbursement benefits. She met all the requirements and took a few classes each semester. Jessica wasn't happy at her job. Instead of viewing it with a negative eye, she changed her perspective and appreciated all the benefits available to her. Jessica planned to work for the corporation until they paid off her tuition and then use her education and skills to pursue her true passion. A few years later, she earned her degree with little to no student loan debt. She did everything required of her employer until she could leave the company and embark on her new journey.

# HEALTH INSURANCE / DISABILITY COVERAGE

Employers who offer health insurance will split the cost of premiums with you. Health insurance provides financial protection if you have a severe illness or accident. Disability coverage could pay a considerable portion of your salary if you're unable to work.

Several years ago, my doctor recommended I get surgery. I did so because I had healthcare benefits through my employer, and I knew it wouldn't put a massive dent in my finances. Having health insurance saved me from having medical debt. The expenses added up quickly, and there was no way I would have been able to afford the medical bills. I could not work for a little over a month after the surgery. I received up to 60% of my salary each pay period until I could return to work, which helped me sustain my living expenses.

> **Note to reader:** Advice given in this lesson is not intended to influence your decisions about investing or financial products. You should always seek professional guidance that considers your circumstances before making any financial decisions.

> **Note to reader: Instead of complaining, seize every opportunity, small or large, through all steps in your career path.**

78

Pause and take the time to seriously consider what you have just read. Don't rush to the next lesson without reflecting on what you have learned.

# LESSON 5

## INVEST IN YOURSELF

*"Your ideas, dreams, and skills won't become assets*
*until you put them into motion."*
*– Erven Nelson.*

## KEY WORDS

- ❖ Invest
- ❖ Stocks
- ❖ Risky Investor
- ❖ Play-It-Safe Investor

# INTRODUCTION

The greatest assets you possess are time and health. The purpose of this lesson is to help you identify where to spend your time and effort to make something better.

# OBJECTIVES

When you have completed this lesson, you will have learned the following:

1.  Distinguish the difference between a Risky Investor and a Play-it-safe investor.
2.  How to invest in yourself.

## TAKE CALCULATED RISK

The stock market is where investors buy and sell shares of ownership in a company. People who invest in the stock market are referred to as risky investors because their investments have no guaranteed return. Risky investors take calculated risks and are not afraid to fail. They understand there is a 50% chance they could gain a lot of money and a 50% chance of losing it all. Other investors may not invest in the stock market because they are afraid of losing. These are the investors who like to play it safe.

Before I lose you, let's be clear. I'm not suggesting you invest your money in the stock market.

Your skills and ideas are comparable to the stock market because they provide the highest potential returns. However, unlike stocks, they never lose value. It's important to remember that they won't become assets until you put them into motion. Decide if you are a risky investor or an investor that likes to play it safe.

> **Note to reader: Your ideas and skills won't become assets until you put them into motion.**

# RISKY INVESTORS

Risky investors are not afraid to invest in their skills and ideas despite the possibility of taking a considerable loss. A risky investor will create a plan and take action. Think of all your ideas and skills as stocks. The more you invest in them, the greater the opportunities for you to receive a return. A return can be a pay increase, rewards, self-development, education, etc.

You may be asking yourself, "Which idea or skill do I invest in first?"

Like the stock market, you invest in the idea or skill with the highest potential returns, the one that you are more passionate about. You must identify what the potential outcomes are. Your brain cannot focus on ten different ideas at once. Fully commit to one idea or skill, master it, and it will make room for the others later on in life.

# PLAY-IT-SAFE INVESTORS

One reason why play-it-safe investors are afraid to invest in themselves is because they fear failure. You will never see a return on your skills and ideas if fear prevents you from taking calculated risks. (Refer to the first lesson to get insights on releasing fear.)

You will fail at some point in your life, but how you react to failure makes the difference. You can view failure with a positive eye or a negative eye. For example, if you fail an exam, you probably didn't completely understand the questions you answered wrong. If you view failing your exam with a negative eye, you will feel defeated and lose hope. To study and still fail might feel like a waste of time. However, if you view failing with a positive eye, you will identify the wrong answers and use them as a study guide to do much better next time. You will recognize where you need improvement and seek help.

Here are a few more examples to help you distinguish the difference between a person with a positive and negative eye:

- ❖ A person with a positive eye identifies opportunities for improvement.
- ❖ A person with a negative eye only sees limitations.
- ❖ A person with a positive eye sees the good in others.
- ❖ A person with a negative eye sees the bad in others.
- ❖ A person with a positive eye looks for solutions.
- ❖ A person with a negative eye makes excuses and looks for problems.

# INVEST IN YOURSELF

Spend your time and money developing your mind by continuously reading educational books to build your knowledge and listening to motivational audiobooks or podcasts to push yourself to reach higher. Take long, thoughtful walks and think about who you are, what you want to become, and how you will get there.

I prefer mantra meditation whenever I need to clear my head. Mantra meditation is a meditation approach that uses phrases (mantras) to help you focus and clear your mind. I was introduced to this method by a coworker who meditated regularly. I usually find a quiet corner in my house or office and repeat, "I am blessed" until I feel relaxed. You could also seek therapy or exercise.

You may not have the team to facilitate your ideas yet, but you can start preparing yourself today with the expectation that opportunities could arrive tomorrow. One way to do this is by attending workshops and seminars to expand your network with like-minded people. Seek coaches and mentors as early as you can who will challenge you to step outside your comfort zone so you can move forward in life. Find people who will help you see your value.

We live in a social media culture where everything happens so quickly, causing us to expect instant gratification. We want everything to happen the instant we desire it. For most of us, this isn't reality. It will take time to reach your desired results when you invest in yourself. Set attainable goals and make small progress every day (refer to the second lesson to get insights on setting achievable goals). You must cultivate patience and discipline. Don't get discouraged when you cannot build your business to a Fortune 500 company overnight.

> **Note to reader: You may not have the team to facilitate your ideas yet, but you can start preparing yourself today with the expectation that opportunities could arrive tomorrow.**

Looking back, I remember commuting 40 minutes to and from work five days a week, which equaled 400 minutes. When I decided I wanted to take charge of my own life, I committed to using those 400 minutes spent in my car listening to audiobooks, podcasts, and YouTube content that inspired me to reach the next level in my life. In total, 400 minutes each week multiplied by 52 weeks in a calendar year is a minimum of 20,800 minutes of free education. Today, investing time in my personal growth has become a habit. Twenty thousand eight hundred minutes doesn't nearly compare to the time I spend in a calendar year. Whether I'm on a lunch break at work, walking my dog, on vacation, in my car, or at the gym, I always find opportunities to listen to audiobooks, podcasts, or YouTube content related to my top priorities.

In the boxes below, list four trades or skills you possess that have value and potential. Now put them in order by priority. Prioritize what matters to you. What's your purpose? Write the most important one in the first box. If you play an instrument, write "musician," or "auto mechanic" if you repair or maintain vehicles.

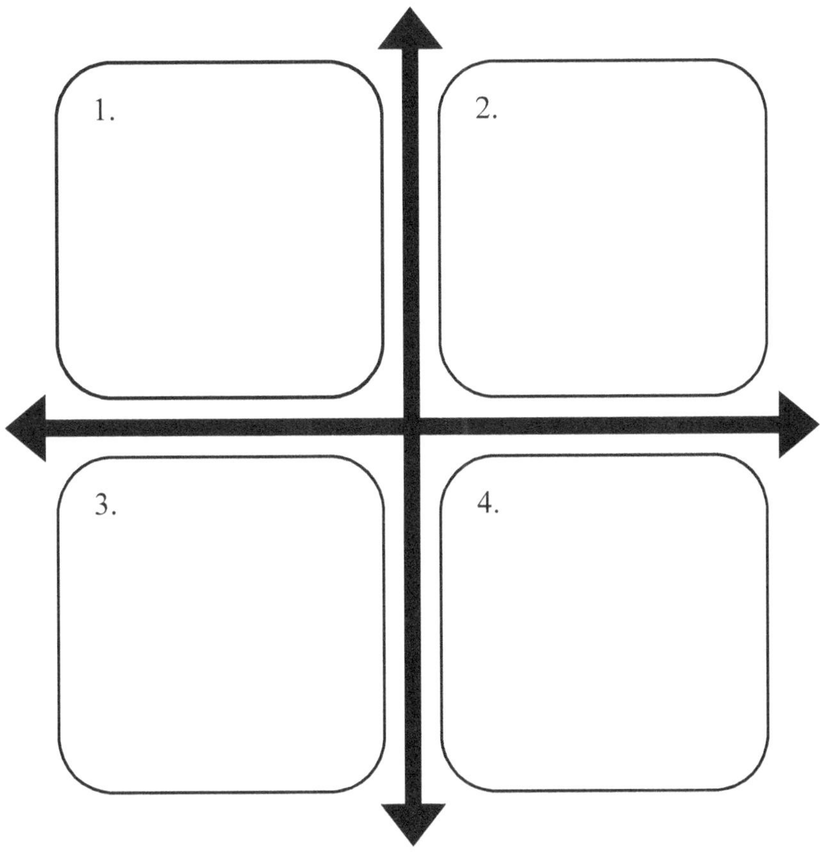

For the next 30 days, read at least one book related to that priority. If you prefer audio, you could listen to podcasts or YouTube content related to your focus for a minimum of 30 minutes each day. The goal is to help you organize your goals by priorities and provide you with the habit-building tool you need to reach your desired results.

After 30 days, evaluate. Don't practice every priority at once. After completing this challenge, you can move to the next priority box and repeat the process.

Pause and take the time to seriously consider what you have just read. Don't rush to the next lesson without reflecting on what you have learned.

# LESSON 6

## POWER OF NETWORKING

*"You will get all you want in life if you help
enough people get what they want."*
*– Zig Ziglar*

## KEY WORDS

- ❖ Network
- ❖ Credibility

# INTRODUCTION

Over the years, when I thought of networking, I imagined salespeople dressed in suits, shaking hands and handing out business cards promoting a product or brand. Chances are, you can relate to that perspective. I quickly discovered that my view was wrong when I started networking myself. I want to address the attitude I had to develop to build relationships with people that landed more opportunities in my personal and professional life. This lesson will teach you critical principles of networking that will help you make better connections.

# OBJECTIVES

When you have completed this lesson, you will have learned how to do the following:

- ❖ Establish how to build your network.
- ❖ Be present.
- ❖ Create a trusting environment.
- ❖ Initiate a conversation.
- ❖ Add value to others.
- ❖ Connect your contacts.

# HOW TO BUILD YOUR NETWORK

Some people primarily focus on how they can help develop long-term relationships and mutual benefits in their network. Others primarily focus on benefiting from people in their network; their objective is to gain as many new consumers as possible. Then, of course, some show up to a networking event and don't network at all. You must develop the mentality that one connection could significantly change your entire life, no matter how many times you get turned down. Instead of complaining, you have to address the situation positively and keep building relationships. That has to be your constant attitude when trying to build your network. I will teach you the exact process I use and teach others who want to try an approach that builds genuine sustainable relationships.

### 1. Be Present

❖ Get out and meet people in person and never slow your momentum. Being present may be one of the most significant investments you can make.

❖ Be surrounded by people who encourage your ideas and support your ambitions.

❖ Make a challenging sacrifice. Some people create a list of excuses and rationalize why they couldn't attend a networking event. You will have to sacrifice hanging out with friends or watching your favorite TV series on a Friday or Saturday night to be present at local networking events that relate to your target audience, but it will be worth it in the long run. If you are an introvert or feel drained when around large crowds, I suggest focusing on a small goal to initialize a conversation with one person in a social setting. This new habit will ensure a little progress in getting you more comfortable engaging in larger crowds.

## 2. Create a Trusting Environment

❖ Build credibility. One way to build credibility is by listening and showing you care.

❖ Put the best interest of others before your own.

❖ Ask for advice and offer helpful feedback.

❖ Don't pretend you know more than you do.

❖ Keep your word and follow through on the task you commit to accomplishing. If you fail to meet a promise, more than likely, they will lose confidence in you.

## 3. Initiate Conversation

❖ Before the event, identify people who can help you get to a connection you don't have. Use social media tools such as Facebook, Instagram, Twitter, and LinkedIn to browse their profile to see if you share the same passions. Taking this extra step will better prepare you to initiate a conversation. Don't wait for them to approach you when you arrive at the event. Read the room well and react appropriately. One way to engage is by making eye contact, smiling, and acknowledging people within a 5-foot radius of you.

❖ Ask questions such as "What problem do you have that needs to be solved?" and then solve it for them.

## 4. Add Value to Others

- ❖ Genuinely show interest in other people's goals.
- ❖ Ask how you can assist them with accomplishing their goals. Offer your expertise in areas where they struggle. Think of creative ways to drive improvement for their needs.
- ❖ Volunteer your time and energy to build closer relationships.

## 5. Connect Your Contacts

- ❖ Refer your contacts to other people. Don't always think about yourself! If you know someone who can fulfill the wants or needs of others, refer them. When you add value to people in your network, there is a chance they will introduce you to their contacts.

My life has been full of opportunity and mentorship. I have developed meaningful relationships that contributed significantly to my growth. The power of networking is real, and executing these principles can make a real difference in your life.

I remember engaging a customer at work that led to a conversation about driving change in our community. Let's call him Bob. I expressed how passionate I was about mentoring young adults and how I aspired to impact society positively. Bob mentioned running for commissioner in the local community and invited me to give a motivational speech at his campaign event. I had never done a speaking engagement before, but I wouldn't let that stop me. I accepted his invitation and showed no sign of hesitation. I would have never imagined my first speaking engagement to be at a campaign event. I practiced speaking in front of friends, family, and the small mirror in my bathroom until I got comfortable speaking.

On the day of the campaign event, I was comfortable and well prepared for my first motivational speech about contributing to positive change in the community. I did not ask Bob for compensation. However, I offered my time and service to fit his needs. After the event, Bob introduced me to the president of the Rotary Club in our community. He was impressed by my speech and invited me to be his guest at a board meeting. He connected me with several community leaders who were equally passionate about impacting positive change in the community. Suddenly, my community network went from 0 to 100! If I hadn't challenged myself to engage Bob (a random customer), worked countless hours to prepare an impactful speech, and been present at the event, I would not have landed the incredible opportunities that came along the way. I offered my skills and recourses to help someone else and made a lot of relationships in return.

# NETWORKING ACTIVITY

In the columns below, let's take inventory of the people you interact with most. Examples of people you could list are friends, family, partners, suppliers, supporters, colleagues, vendors, spouses, mentors, and investors.

|  |  |
|---|---|
|  |  |
|  |  |
|  |  |
|  |  |
|  |  |
|  |  |
|  |  |
|  |  |
|  |  |

2. Ask yourself the following questions:

- ❖ Do they add value to my life?
- ❖ Do they support my ambitions, goals, or dreams?

If you answered no to anyone written in the columns, consider reducing your footprint with them to be at your best for yourself, your loved ones, and your business.

3. After taking inventory of the people you interact with the most and identifying the ones you answered yes to the questions above, assess your relationship with them. This challenge requires both honesty and deep self-reflection.

Ask yourself the following questions about the people listed in the columns:

- ❖ How can I help fulfill their needs with my skills, trades, time, or other resources?
- ❖ Do I add value to our relationship?
- ❖ Do I support their ambitions, goals, or dreams?

4. Now it's time to make it right. For example, if there is someone valuable to you, and through the challenge you find you're not valuing the relationship, ask yourself, "what can I do to reciprocate value to this person?" Write down your thoughts in the box below.

Pause and take the time to seriously consider what you have just read. Don't rush to the next lesson without reflecting on what you have learned.

# LESSON 7

## BASIC FINANCIAL LITERACY

*"I've never been poor, only broke. Being poor is a frame of mind. Being broke is only a temporary situation."*
*– Michael Todd*

*"You will never know true freedom until you achieve financial freedom."*
*- Robert Kiyosaki*

# KEY WORDS

- Debt
- Assets
- Bad Debt
- Credit
- Liabilities
- Compound interest
- Tax exemption
- Emergency fund
- Good Debt
- Growth
- Debt to income ratio (RTI)
- Investment account
- Tax
- Gross income
- Cash flow
- Ring of wealth
- Simple Interest
- Leverage
- Inflation
- Charitable
- Loss
- Net income
- Rule of 72
- Life insurance
- Rate of return
- Profit

**Note to Reader**

The information in this lesson is for educational and informational purposes only. I am not a financial advisor. Do not take anything in this lesson as financial advice, investment advice, trading advice, or other advice. The information in this lesson is based on my personal experiences and is not specific to you. Do your research.

You should not make any decision, financial, investment, trading, or otherwise, based on any of the information presented in this lesson without doing your research and consulting with a professional investment advisor, broker, or financial advisory.

# INTRODUCTION

It's tough to make ends meet. It seems the more you earn, the more you spend, and you can never get ahead. Maybe your salary is growing, but you do not have money left after paying all your bills. You want to start saving, but you are confused about if you should pay off your debt first. You do not know where to start.

I know the feeling. At the age of twenty-five, my income was enough to pay my monthly bills with one check. I got four paychecks each month on top of a monthly bonus, and I was still not getting ahead. I didn't begin to see a positive change in my finances until I focused on where my money was going. This experience created a desire to share what I have learned to help you plan and make good financial decisions.

The purpose of this lesson is to provide you with essential financial language and principles that will teach you the fundamentals of how money works.

# OBJECTIVES

When you have completed this lesson, you will have learned the following:

- The ring of debt
- Assets vs. liabilities
- Bad debt vs. good debt
- Debt to income ratio (DTI)
- The ring of wealth
- Rate of return
- Cash flow
- Profits & losses
- Basics of inflation
- Life insurance
- Simple interest vs. compound interest
- Multiple streams of passive income
- Basics of taxes and tax exemption
- Being charitable

## THE RING OF DEBT

Marketing corporations have convinced you to purchase more than what you earn. It's like people must buy everything they see. I call it "The Ring of Debt."

Here's how it works:

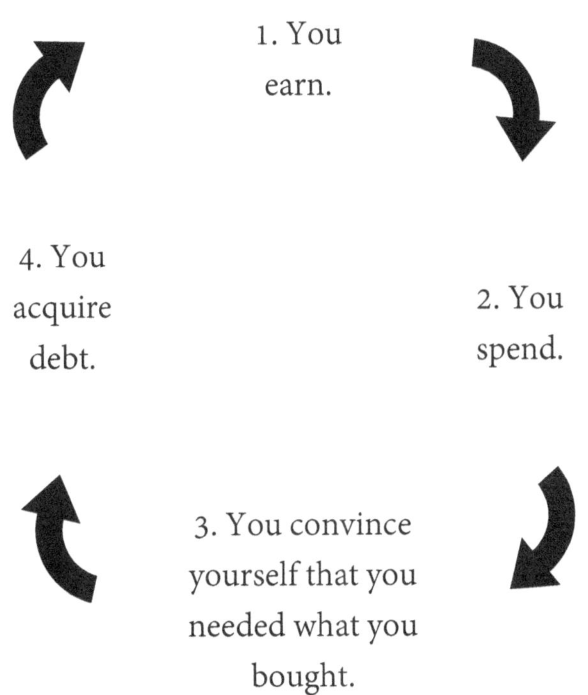

Are you ready to take control of your retirement? Avoid joining those approaching retirement with little to no savings. Your parents' good or bad money habits are not an excuse for how you handle your money. Only you can choose to be financially literate. I recommend you put your "Ego Left" aside and redesign your character from poor thinking to rich thinking. (Refer back to the first lesson of the book to learn more about ego.)

Broke people stay broke, and rich people get richer because the rich understand financial literacy, and broke people do not. A rich man can lose a million dollars, start with nothing, and earn a million dollars again because he understands how money works.

# ASSETS VS. LIABILITIES

If you want to earn money, you must understand the difference between an asset and a liability. Assets are resources that make you money, while liabilities take away from your income. The goal is to minimize your liabilities and grow your assets. Think of liabilities like debt and assets like potential economic resources.

# BAD DEBT VS. GOOD DEBT

What is debt?

> Webster dictionary defines debt as a state of being under obligation to repay someone or something in return for something received: a state of owing.

If you are making recurring payments to someone, it is considered debt.

Bad debt is borrowing money for something that depreciates or won't produce more income.

**Examples of bad debt:**

1.) Single Family Home
2.) Automobile Loan
3.) Student Loans
4.) Credit Cards

Good debt is borrowing money that has the potential to increase your revenue over time.

**Examples of good debt:**

1.) Rental Property (earning income greater than the monthly installments)
2.) Automobile Loan (used as a taxi service earning income greater than the monthly installments)
3.) Student Loans (to obtain education)
4.) Business Loans (to launch and or grow your business)

Use leverage to take advantage of the bank's money. In the examples below, I will show you how to convert bad debt into good debt.

**Examples of bad debt converted into good debt:**

1.) Residential property loans can be good debt if you plan to rent the property out to earn residual income or acquire a residence with potential equity. Say your mortgage is $1,000 a month, but you rent out the entire property for $1,500 a month. The property is an asset because it's making you an extra $500 a month. You are purchasing an asset that retains some value, providing that the interest plus principal is affordable. It enables you to buy an expensive investment before saving for the whole amount. Another example of converting a residential property into good debt is hosting your property with companies like Airbnb.

2.) Automobiles are needed to get you to and from work, but the interest rate is a waste of money. The vehicle depreciates the moment you drive off the car lot. Purchase the least expensive, most reliable vehicle and pay it off quickly. You can convert your car into an asset by renting it out or turning your vehicle into an independent taxi service with Uber or Lyft. Another example of converting your automobile into an investment is building a small car-sharing business with companies like Turo.

3.) Student loans are a liability, but education is an asset. The more education you have, the greater your potential to earn money. If you don't finish school or pass your classes, it would be considered a liability because you will have student loan debt without having learned anything. Educators and first responders go through years of study and acquire large sums of debt, but they are passionate about working in their field.

How do you want your life to look?

Some people find happiness in simply going to work every day. Don't feel discouraged if you have student loan debt; plan to pay it off in small installments. Remember that you are building an investment into a career and a future in education.

4.) Credit cards can be a source of good debt if you build a good credit history. You can leverage your good credit history to get approved for the items listed in the "examples of good debt" section above. The longer you have been using your credit, the better. Don't overspend, and most importantly, pay your bills on time. Don't make large purchases with your credit card that you can't afford to pay back in a timely fashion. With good credit history, you can leverage your credit to purchase a home, start a business, or purchase a vehicle with low interest rates. If you desire to purchase a vehicle, I prefer purchasing an inexpensive, reliable car with cash or one that you can pay off quickly.

You are probably asking, "How can I establish credit with a poor credit history?"

One way to build credit is by applying for a secured credit card. Deposit money into a secured credit card account, and your credit limit will equal that amount. Make consistent payments on time to avoid paying any interest. Over time, your credit score will increase tremendously. The goal is to pull from your line of credit to assess opportunities without selling your assets.

For example, I deposited $400.00 into a secured credit card account, so my credit limit equaled that amount. My credit score improved over three months because I made consistent payments. I avoided paying high interest rates by making payments before the deadline and not exhausting more than 30% of the limit. Eventually, I was offered credit cards from other banks because I had established good credit history.

# DEBT TO INCOME RATIO (DTI)

Now that you have a better understanding of debt, let's figure out your debt to income ratio. Your debt to income ratio is all your monthly payments divided by your monthly income after taxes.

Example: Let's say you make $2,500 a month after taxes.

1.) What is the total of your monthly recurring payments?

**Example**: Car loan, rent, student loans, insurance, and phone bill add up to about $1,500 a month.

$$1,500 / 2,500 = 0.60$$

As a result, 60% of your monthly income after taxes pays your monthly debts. What are you doing with the other 40% of your earnings? With every dollar bill you earn, you have the power to determine where it goes. You can misspend it on liabilities and become poor or spend it wisely on assets and become wealthy.

# THE RING OF WEALTH

I created the "The Ring of Wealth" to help you manage and grow your income by closely monitoring your spending and saving habits. It's time to get out of "The Ring of Debt" and join "The Ring of Wealth."

## THE RING OF WEALTH:

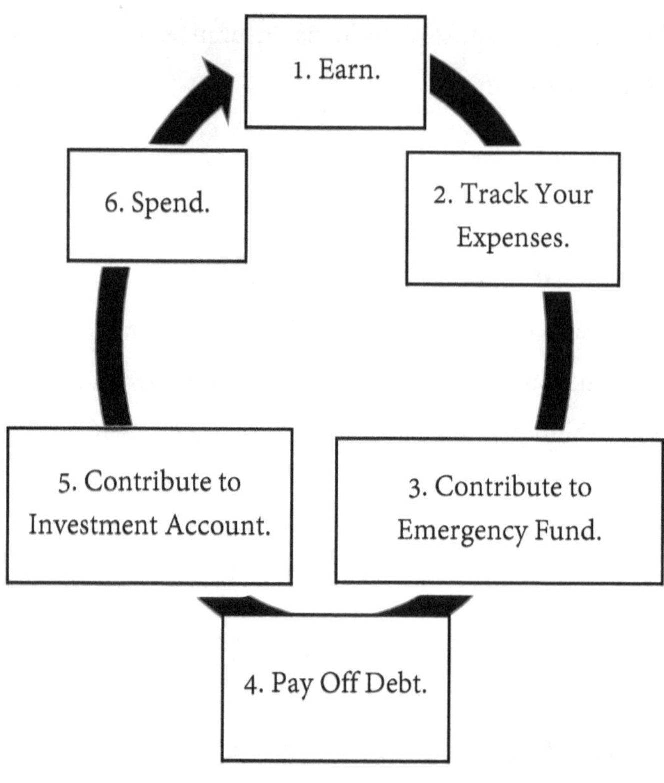

# THE RING OF WEALTH STEP 1: EARN

If you are unemployed, you should find work immediately. Allow your curiosity to lead you into new information to see if it's right for you. If you are working for an employer that hasn't terminated you for poor performance, you probably have a skill you don't realize you have. Otherwise, they would have fired you. Sometimes when you work on a trade long enough, you don't realize how much you are developing in that area. It becomes a part of your behavior. Eventually, you get so good at it that your boss offers you a pay raise or promotion.

Some complain that their job is taking advantage of them but doesn't recognize that their employer sees more value in their skills than they see in themselves. Imagine what you could accomplish if you believed in yourself more than your employer. You would probably venture off into entrepreneurship using those same skills and earn a fortune. Whether you are working for an employer or self-employed, you must find work and make money now. Whatever it is you do, become a master at it. Keep working on improving your skills. Ask yourself, how can I add value to others and get paid to do it?

One day, my mother said I should get a job. I was a senior in high school with no clue what I wanted to do after graduation. I did know that I had to start earning money to get the things I desired in life. I had no savings and no financial education. I remember taking two hours on a typical hot Florida day to walk up and down the busy main street, stopping business to business, to inquire if they were hiring. I didn't have a car, and I had no money for the bus fare.

Frustration grew inside me and my patience dwindled, but the grind did not stop. I received many "no's" before I got one "yes" that changed my life.

My mindset had to be, "I'll get the next one." Getting the job in a highly known franchise in the United States of America was very memorable. The job was so important to me because I could positively impact the economic struggles within my family. My friends viewed summer as a time to hang out and relax, but I worked over 40 hours each week instead.

One year of devoted service led to my first car, my first apartment, and having the opportunity to earn my own money. The lesson I learned through this experience was that no one owed me anything. No one was coming to save my family from our economic struggles. If I wanted a better lifestyle, I had to get up early, break some sweat walking up and down the busy street, embrace a lot of "no's," and work extremely hard.

TIP: How to Prepare for an Interview

Based on my five years of experience as a hiring manager, here are the top five things recruiters and employers look for in candidates:

### 1. DO NOT Arive Late

- ❖ Arrive 10 minutes before the interview to anticipate traffic, weather, and loss in direction. It will also give you time to collect your thoughts and mentally prepare.
- ❖ Early arrival will show employers that you are responsible and possess good time-management skills.

### 2. Let Your Personality Shine

- ❖ Greet your interviewer with a friendly smile.
- ❖ Let your personality shine! In some cases, your credentials will not earn you a job opportunity if your personality does not fit their

culture and team. Unfortunately, if you and another equally qualified candidate exceeded expectations during an interview, but there is only one position available for the role, the employer will pick the person they liked the most. The key is getting the interviewer to like you as a person just as they want your skills and experience.

### 3. Be Confident

- Think of an interview as just a conversation between you and the interviewer. Avoid stuttering and long pauses.
- Maintain eye contact and practice good body language.
- Try to be relaxed, but use a passionate communication style. One way to build your confidence is to conduct practice interviews in the same format as the real one. For example, if it's a face to face interview, ask a friend to meet and conduct a mock interview with you to practice answering questions in person. Choose a friend who is willing to give you honest feedback.
- Practice looking in the mirror and answering sample questions out loud.

### 4. Be Prepared

- Bring extra copies of your resume to the interview.
- Be ready to share highlights of your career journey for a minimum of five minutes.
- Prepare 2-3 questions to ask the interviewer.
- Make sure your clothes are ironed, clean, and presentable.

## 5. Use The SAPL Method

The **SAPL** method is a technique you can use to answer behavioral-based interview questions by discussing the situation, action, positive result of the situation you are describing, and the lesson learned during the process.

- ❖ **Situation**: Describe the situation first.
- ❖ **Actions**: Identify the steps you took to handle the situation.
- ❖ **Positive Result**: What were the results of your actions? Keep it positive. Avoid using a situation with a negative outcome. Talk about some numbers, percentages, or increases you can use when talking about your responsibilities and accomplishments.
- ❖ **Lesson Learned**: Give an example of a lesson you learned that didn't interfere with your ability to get the job done. Did the experience grow your skills?

**SAPL Example:**

Question: Tell me about a time you went above and beyond for a customer.

**Situation:**

One time, at my last retail job, an elderly customer who I had never seen before struggled to carry groceries in one hand while holding a cane in the other for balance and support while walking.

**Actions:**

First, I stopped the tasks I was performing at the time to acknowledge the customer immediately. Then, I asked for her name and offered to free up her hands from the shopping basket she was carrying instead of waiting for her to ask for help. She expressed that she was feeling muscle aches and fatigue but needed to buy a few grocery items for her grandkids visiting on the next calendar day. With her permission, I wrapped her arm around my shoulder to assist her in walking to her vehicle. I gave the customer a pen and paper to write a grocery list and offered to do the shopping for her. I wanted to ensure that someone else was fulfilling my role and adhering to the business needs, so I communicated with other team members over a headset that I would be spending additional time shopping for the customer. Finally, I loaded the groceries into her vehicle and thanked her for choosing to shop at my store instead of local competitors.

**Positive Result:**

The customer completed a survey explaining how she had an exceptional experience, contributing to positive store metrics. The customer is currently a regular customer who visits several times weekly, which is essential to sales and profit growth.

**Lesson Learned:**

The lesson from the scenario was that going the extra mile to make a customer's day leads to business success. Growing sales starts with the experience the customer receives in any business establishment. Since then, I've been striving to make someone's day a little brighter, inside and outside of work.

# THE RING OF WEALTH STEP 2:
# TRACK YOUR EXPENSES

It is crucial to create an expense sheet to help monitor your money. Ask yourself, where is my money going? If you are spending less than what you earn every month, you are off to a great start! However, if you spend more than you make monthly, you need to cut back. Tell your money where to go instead of wondering.

For example, John's monthly net income is $1,920 working in a fast-food corporation. John is concerned that he works so much but always feels broke. In the expense sheet below, John will list his monthly expenses and determine if he is managing his money responsibly or poorly.

> **Note:** Net income is your take-home pay. Gross income is what employees earn before taxes, benefits, and other payroll deductions withheld from their wages.

| John's Expense Sheet | |
|---|---|
| Monthly Net Income | $1,920 |
| **Monthly Expenses** | |
| Rent + Water | $950 |
| Internet | $60 |
| Electric | $50 |
| Car payment | $220 |
| Car insurance | $190 |
| Music subscription | $10 |
| Movie streaming subscription | $10 |
| Phone plan | $80 |
| Gym subscription | $20 |
| Eating out | $240 |
| Fuel | $80 |
| Fit club subscription | $10 |
| Tobacco | $50 |
| Social events | $40 |
| **Total** | $2,010 |

John is now aware of his poor spending habits, so he cuts back.

In John's updated expense sheet below, you will see how tracking your expenses and living below your means can help you manage your money.

| John's Updated Expense Sheet | |
| --- | --- |
| Monthly Net Income | $1,920 |
| **Monthly Expenses** | |
| Rent + Water | $950 |
| Internet | $60 |
| Electric | $50 |
| Car payment | $220 |
| Car insurance | $190 |
| ~~Music subscription~~ | ~~$10~~ |
| ~~Movie streaming subscription~~ | ~~$10~~ |
| ~~Phone plan~~<br>Pre-paid plan | ~~$80~~<br>$30 |
| ~~Gym subscription~~<br>Work-out at home | ~~$20~~<br>$0 |
| ~~Eating out~~<br>Grocery shopping/packed lunch | ~~$240~~<br>$160 |
| Fuel | $80 |
| ~~Fit club subscription~~ | ~~$10~~ |
| ~~Tobacco~~ | ~~$50~~ |
| ~~Social events~~ | ~~$40~~ |
| **Total** | $1,740 |

List your monthly net income and expected expenses on the following expense sheet below to help you track your spending habits.

## My Expense Sheet

| | | |
|---|---|---|
| Monthly Net Income | | $ |

| Monthly Expenses | Due Date | Total |
|---|---|---|
| | | $ |
| | | $ |
| | | $ |
| | | $ |
| | | $ |
| | | $ |
| | | $ |
| | | $ |
| | | $ |
| | | $ |
| | | $ |
| | | $ |
| | | $ |
| | | $ |
| | | $ |
| | | $ |
| | | $ |
| | | $ |
| | Total | $ |

Subtract your monthly expenses from your monthly net income. The balance is what's left over after all costs are covered every month.

| | | |
|---|---|---|
| Monthly Gross Income (MGI) | | $ |
| Monthly Expenses (ME) | | $ |
| Balance (B) | | $ |

I remember living paycheck to paycheck through my first semester in college. I felt as if my life only consisted of working and studying. I couldn't afford to hang out with friends, and I struggled to pay my bills. When someone would ask if I wanted to meet at a pricey restaurant with tablecloths, I would respond, "I don't have an appetite" or "I'm on a strict diet." I would find any excuse not to attend an event involving spending money. One day, I decided to change my spending habits and control my finances. I wanted to know where every penny that left my bank account was going. I started tracking my expenses in the "Notes" application on my smartphone. It looked something like this:

## 2014 Monthly Expenses

Rent: Due on the 1st - $750.00

Car Insurance: Due on the 2nd - $210.00

Car Payment: Due on the 2nd - $225.00

Gym Subscription: Due on the 6th - $20.00

Phone Bill: Due on the 9th - $110.00

Subscription 1: Due on the 13th - $13.00

Subscription 2: Due on the 14th - $10.00

This format worked for me at the time, but eventually, as my list grew, I recognized that I needed a more organized and simplified system. I immediately saw better results when I developed the "Expense Sheet" to track my expenses.

# THE RING OF WEALTH STEP 3: EMERGENCY FUND

Contributing a portion of your earnings into an emergency bank account is a smart way to prepare for unexpected life events. Think of it as an insurance policy. The first step is to get started, even if only a tiny amount, and to gradually increase your contribution over time.

An emergency fund is money set aside to cover unexpected financial surprises. This might be a car accident, medical issue, loss of employment, a tree falling on your house, or your car breaking down. It's not a matter of if, but when a financial emergency occurs. I would rather my financial surprises be annoying to pay (but I have the money to cover it) rather than a tragedy. Set your emergency fund goal to a minimum of 3 months' expenses.

Multiply your net income by 10% to calculate your emergency fund contribution on each pay period.

> **TIP:** Once your paycheck hits your checking account, it's a good idea to have your bank account set to automatically send 10% from your checking account to your emergency fund.

In 2019, I was driving home from work around 11:30 PM, exhausted after my eight-hour shift. The weather was clear, and there was no traffic. As I passed through a green light turning left, I noticed a bright headlight on my driver-side window. Before I could grasp what was happening, my vehicle was struck on the left rear-end by an oncoming car.

After the impact, I gripped the steering wheel, attempting to gain control, but I was unsuccessful. Thankfully, no one else was in my vehicle and the airbags did not hit me. I got out of the car to make sure the other person was okay, but the other vehicle was gone. I had been involved in a hit-and-run. The impact had me so shaken up that I didn't know what to think.

I hadn't seen the license plate or make and model of the vehicle that hit me. I felt lower back pain at the time, but I had no visible wounds and none of my bones were broken. I was grateful to be alive. When the police officers arrived on the scene, they told me they hadn't located the other driver involved in the accident.

Fast forward a few weeks later, my paid-off vehicle was a total loss. Utilizing my emergency fund, I was in a financial position to afford Uber services to commute to and from work for a few weeks until I found my next car. I focused on a solution without the stress of having reliable transportation. One of the lessons I learned in this situation was to always have an emergency fund. I think a lot of people felt that need during the COVID period too.

# THE RING OF WEALTH STEP 4: PAY OFF DEBT

List all of your debts except your mortgage and start to pay off one at a time. When you're in debt with your mortgage, you decide when to pay the money back. When you're in credit card debt, the lender chooses when you have to pay it back. Keep in mind that the mortgage interest costs can be tax-deductible, so the government can help out by lowering your tax bill. Pick the debt with the highest interest rate first and eliminate it. Once the high-interest debt is paid off (credit cards, student loans, etc.), you will have extra money to increase the dollar amount on monthly payments for other debt.

Pay your mortgage off early. If you have a 30-year mortgage at 4% interest for $300,000, your monthly payment is $1,432.25. Suppose you put an additional $400 into these payments with the same term, principal, and interest rate. You can pay off your mortgage in approximately 19 years and two months. You would eliminate almost 11 years of debt, saving you roughly $81,099.00 in interest. So if you have extra money lying around, pay more toward your principal.

# THE RING OF WEALTH STEP 5: INVESTMENT ACCOUNT

Now that you have your emergency fund set aside and debt paid off, it's a good idea to save up at least 10% of your earnings each pay period in your investment account. Think of it as paying yourself first. If you pay yourself first today, you will accumulate significant assets for your future. An investment account is money set aside to invest in assets. Assets can be your business ideas, skills, education, or training. Let's say you are an up-and-coming recording artist. You could use the investment account to invest in studio time, music production, videos, or marketing for your new song. (Refer back to the "Invest in Yourself" lesson to discover where you could invest your money.) The contribution amount depends on your investment goals and timeframe. Remember, investing is how you keep the money you earn.

One advantage of having an investment account is that you decide how to allocate your funds.

It is crucial to have the emergency fund established first because if things beyond your control go wrong, you could lose the money in the investment account. Consider seeking advice from someone who has proved that they know what they're doing.

> **TIP:** Once your paycheck hits your checking account, it's a good idea to have your bank account set to automatically send 10% from your checking account to your investment account electronically.

# THE RING OF WEALTH STEP 6: SPEND

*"Don't save what is left after spending; spend*
*what is left after saving."*
*– Warren Buffet.*

You started earning money in step 1 and began tracking your expenses in step 2; created a savings account in step 3 and paid off your debt in step 4. In step 5, you began contributing to your investment account. So here in step 6, you can spend your remaining balance on non-essentials. When you make it to this step, you can take the vacation you always dreamed of or take your partner to a pricey restaurant, one with a tablecloth.

### Rate of Return

The Rule of 72 is a formula that estimates the number of years it takes to double your investment value, given a fixed annual rate of return. It's a fundamental formula that anyone can use to calculate the effect of compound interest on building wealth.

Take 72 and divide it by the annual interest rate to get the number of years it will take to double your money.

**For example**: With 3% interest

72 / 3 = 24 years to double your money

## The Rule of 72

**72 / 3 = 24**

Money doubles every 24 years

| AGE | 3% |
|---|---|
| 25 | $5,000 |
| 49 | $10,000 |
| 73 | $15,000 |

## Cash Flow

Cash flow is how much revenue is coming into your business. Cash flow will show how much cash is entering the business and money leaving the company.

### Profit & Loss

Profit is revenue minus expenses. When a company produces money for shareholders and builds a structure that will guarantee positive returns for years to come, it means the company has a cash flow.

**Positive cash flow example:**

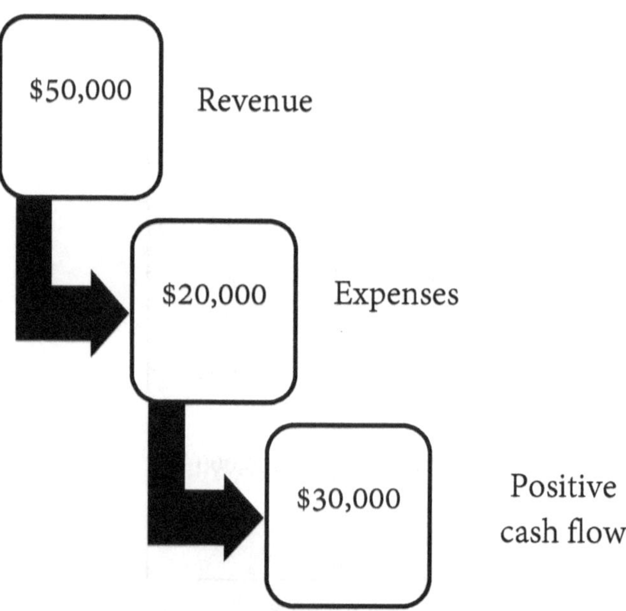


**$50,000 (revenue) - $20,000 (expenses) = $30,000 (positive cash flow)**

Loss is if a company is accumulating more debt than profit. It means that the company has a negative cash flow.

**Negative cash flow example:**

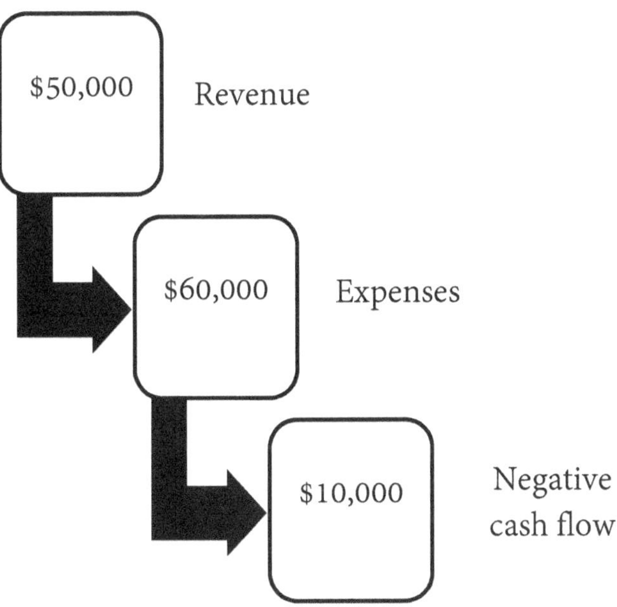


**$50,000 (revenue) - $60,000 (expenses) = -$10,000 (negative cash flow)**

The goal is to invest in assets to accumulate a positive cash flow.

## Growth

The more cash flow you produce, the more you should develop unique ways to grow your business. It's one of the most important lessons to sustain wealth. Set a new goal for every milestone you achieve.

## Basics of Inflation

Inflation is the rise in the prices of goods and services over time. Some people don't realize that their 401(k) account is tied to the market. When the market hits hard, so will your retirement investments. Food costs, new vehicle purchase prices, and home prices are rising globally, and the U.S. dollar keeps getting weaker. The cost of living is becoming more expensive, while minimum wages are not enough for living standards.

## Life Insurance

Have you thought about what you will leave behind financially for your family after you die? Life insurance can help you build generational wealth. I know it can be a challenging conversation with your partner or kids, but I believe it's critical to their success. For example, let's say you invested 5x your salary into life insurance. You will leave $150,000 to your beneficiary when you die. Your beneficiary can use the money for whatever purpose they choose. Reach out to a trusted professional to learn more and get started.

# SIMPLE INTEREST VS. COMPOUND INTEREST

## Simple Interest

If you have $100 and earn 5%, you now have $105 after the first year. That 5% applies to your original $100 each year.

Year 1: $100 x 5% = 5

Total: $105

Year 2: $100 x 5% = 5

Total: $110

| YEAR | 5% INTEREST |
|:---:|:---:|
| 1 | $105 |
| 2 | $110 |
| 3 | $115 |
| 4 | $120 |
| 5 | $125 |

## Compound Interest

If you have $100 and earn 5%, you now have $105 after the first year. Then, 5% gets applied to the combined principal plus interest for the following year's calculation.

Year 1: $100 x 5% = 5
Total: $105

Year 2: $105 x 5% = 5.25
Total: $110.25

| YEAR | 5% INTEREST |
| --- | --- |
| 1 | $105 |
| 2 | $110.25 |
| 3 | $115.76 |
| 4 | $121.52 |
| 5 | $127.59 |

# MULTIPLE STREAMS OF PASSIVE INCOME

Multiple streams of passive income are the secret to building wealth. Passive income requires something upfront, such as time or money, to earn you consistent revenue, requiring minimum work to maintain. With passive income, you will be able to make money while you sleep, work your 9-to-5, and while you're on vacation with your family.

### Examples of passive income:

- ❖ Purchase a rental property, hire a property manager to maintain it, and rent it out for more than your monthly payments.
- ❖ Start a YouTube channel and get eligible for monetization. YouTube will monetize your content, and you will earn revenue based on clicks and impressions.
- ❖ Sell a digital product—something you can create once and sell multiple times. Examples are music, ebooks, and courses.

# BASICS OF TAXES AND TAX EXEMPTION

Taxes finance the common good so that everyone can benefit. Taxes fund public services. You pay taxes on any income you obtain according to your ability to pay. You pay a part of the profit as a tax because you used public services to make that profit.

For example, you pay sales tax, income tax, and property tax. "Uncle Sam" will always find a way to benefit from your proceeds.

There are situations when you don't pay taxes; this is called tax exemption. Tax exemption reduces or eliminates your obligation to pay tax.

For example, charities and religious organizations are exempt from paying income tax entirely because they serve the public.

For current tax rates, please visit www.irs.gov.

# BE CHARITABLE

How are you contributing to society?

One key to sustaining wealth is giving. Give from your heart. How often have you heard someone you know say, "When I earn a lot of money, then I will start giving"? Let's be honest; you don't need much money to give. You don't need money at all! There are many forms of giving; you could volunteer your time, share your knowledge and experience with others, or give financially. Some religious people give through tithing. A tithe is a specific amount (10% of your income) that you give first. What they all have in common is contributing to society. Give because you want to show your appreciation, share what you have, and because you care.

Not only can financial recourses be a tax exemption, but they can also help you or your business build significant credibility within the community. It's a win-win!

> **Pause and take the time to consider what you have just read and reflect on what you have learned.**

# BEHIND THE BOOK

When I started to write The 7 L's You Must Take, I wanted to provide the guidance that I wished someone had given my mother when she was twenty-four with six kids. I have a story to share that can offer hope and guidance.

I was raised in challenging environments and through systems designed to keep us in poverty. I slept in shelters with my mother and five siblings. I never really thought that we were poor, or at least I didn't know what that meant, as everyone around us was pretty much the same. Every first week of the month when my mother received EBT, we looked forward to buying whatever groceries we wanted at the grocery store, even the "big brands."

One day, my mother decided to take us on a sight-seeing cruise through affluent neighborhoods with good school districts miles away from where we resided. I will never forget when I realized the world was more extensive than I had known. I remember observing two-story homes that overlooked the water with luxury cars parked in the driveways, a father tossing a baseball to his son on their green manicured lawn, and people playing golf on the community golf courses. My mother gently placed her hand on my arm and said, "One day, you will buy us a house in a neighborhood like this because you are a superstar."

Those were the memories at the root of this book. I have spent my life striving to be "excellent."

It took many years of detoxing and finding myself before developing an excellence mindset. Once I widened my perspective, acquired positive habits aligned with my long-term goals, and learned how money works, I saw progression in my life.

This book is about helping you discover the superstar within and the freedom to live the life you want. It's about teaching you "The 7 L's You Must Take" to succeed financially and reach your fullest potential.

I hope this book helps you develop an excellence mindset and better understand how money works. I hope that it fills you with ferocious gratitude for everything you have accomplished up to now. Because it's less about what we have and more about the legacy we'll leave behind. Ultimately, it's about how we contribute to society while we have the opportunity.

**Note to Mom: Thank you, and I love you.**

# ACKNOWLEDGMENTS

My family, teachers, mentors, and the environments in which I grew up impacted my character, and I will always be grateful.

Thank you also to my editors for assisting me with bringing my first book to life.

To Michael Carragher, thank you for your mentorship, people skills, and competence. You have been an enormous blessing in my life!

To Dacoup Howell, the childhood friend turned brother I never knew I needed, your encouragement has been influential in my journey. Thank you for listening to multiple revisions of the book in the early stages and offering me solutions to do better. You are indeed like a brother to me, and I appreciate you.

To my mom, Sophia Smith, none of this would be possible if it had not been for you raising me to be confident and resilient. I will always be your superstar!

And finally, thank you to my friend, Morgan Nelson, for being such a huge support to me from the very beginning. I owe you an unpayable debt of gratitude.

# CHALLENGES

This part of the book describes eleven challenges that will assist you in translating the insights you have gained (about: finding yourself, setting attainable goals, seizing opportunities, minimizing stress, investing in yourself, the power of networking, and basic financial literacy) into practical skills.

An important note before we dive in: the more complex a particular challenge seems to you, the more potential it contains for your growth.

You will discover that doing the challenges requires a significant amount of time and commitment.

(Erven Nelson's, *The 7 L's You Must Take: Challenge*, is available at: www.iamervennelson.com/challenge)

# CHALLENGE 1: EGO

(review lesson 1)

**Comments:**

This challenge is designed to increase your self-awareness and positively identify your ego.

**Directions:**

1. You have 25 tokens allotted to describe who you are as a character. The number of tokens is less than the number of choices you have to make. Although you may think you possess all of the qualities below, 25 tokens will help you identify which attributes you believe are more important than others. Bubble in the spaces next to each quality to represent what you think of yourself. You must use all 25 tokens.

1. Bubble in the spaces next to each quality to represent what you think of yourself. You must use all 25 tokens.

Attractive ⚬⚬⚬

Intelligent ⚬⚬⚬

Committed ⚬⚬⚬

Loyal ⚬⚬⚬

Funny ⚬⚬⚬

Motivated ⚬⚬⚬

Healthy ⚬⚬⚬

Charitable ⚬⚬⚬

Confident ⚬⚬⚬

Positive ⚬⚬⚬

2. Take the same 25 tokens. In this step, bubble in the spaces next to each quality to represent how others see you. You must use all 25 tokens.

Attractive ○ ○ ○

Intelligent ○ ○ ○

Committed ○ ○ ○

Loyal ○ ○ ○

Funny ○ ○ ○

Motivated ○ ○ ○

Healthy ○ ○ ○

Charitable ○ ○ ○

Confident ○ ○ ○

Positive ○ ○ ○

> **Note:** All of the qualities listed above are positive. You may have rated yourself higher in one attribute than the other, which is okay because a person who sees themselves in a positive light will perform better. When you accurately know yourself, you will make decisions based upon an honest perception of who you are. Ask yourself, "Am I making decisions based on how the world sees me or how I view myself?"

(visit www.iamervennelson.com/challenges to share your results.)

# CHALLENGE 2: THE RING OF WEALTH

(review lesson 7)

**Comments:**

I created the "The Ring of Wealth" to help you manage and grow your income by closely monitoring your spending and saving habits. It's time to get out of the Ring of Debt and join the Ring of Wealth.

**Directions:**

1. **Earn.** Find work and start earning money.
2. **Track your expenses.** List your monthly net income and expected payments on the expense sheet below to help you track your spending habits. Net income is your take-home pay. Gross income is what employees earn before taxes, benefits, and other payroll deductions are withheld from their wages.

My Expense Sheet

| Monthly Net Income | $ |
|---|---|

| Monthly Expenses | Due Date | Total |
|---|---|---|
| | | $ |
| | | $ |
| | | $ |
| | | $ |
| | | $ |
| | | $ |
| | | $ |
| | | $ |
| | | $ |
| | | $ |
| | | $ |
| | | $ |
| | | $ |
| | | $ |
| | | $ |
| | | $ |
| | | $ |
| | Total | $ |

Subtract your monthly expenses from your monthly net income. The balance is what's left over after all costs are covered.

| | | |
|---|---|---|
| Monthly Gross Income (MGI) | | $ |
| Monthly Expenses (ME) | | $ |
| Balance (B) | | $ |

3. **Contribute to an emergency fund**. An emergency fund is monies set aside to cover unexpected financial surprises. Unexpected financial emergencies might be a car accident, medical issue, loss of employment, a tree falling on your house, or your car breaking down. It's not a matter of if, but when a financial emergency occurs.

Set your emergency fund goal to a minimum of 3 months' expenses.

Multiply your net income by 10% to get your emergency fund contribution every time you get paid.

TIP: Once your paycheck hits your checking account, it's a good idea to have your bank account set to automatically send 10% from your checking account to your emergency fund.

4. **Pay off debt**. List all of your debt except for your mortgage. When you're in debt with your mortgage, you decide when to pay the money back. When you're in credit card debt, the lender chooses when you have to pay it back. Keep in mind the mortgage interest costs can be tax-deductible, so the

government can help out by lowering your tax bill. Pick the debt with the highest interest first and eliminate it. Once the high-interest debt is paid off (credit cards, student loans, etc.), you will have extra money to increase the dollar amount on monthly payments for other debt.

> **TIP:** Pay your mortgage off early. If you have a 30-year mortgage at 4% interest for $300,000, your monthly payment is $1,432.25. Suppose you put an additional $400 into these payments with the same term, principal, and interest rate. You can pay off your mortgage in approximately 19 years and two months. You would eliminate almost 11 years of debt, saving you roughly $81,099.00 in interest. So if you have extra money lying around, pay more toward your principal.

5. **Contribute to an investment account**. Now that you have your emergency fund set aside and bad debt paid off, save up at least 10% of your earnings each pay period in your investment account for the long run. An investment account is monies that are aside to invest in assets. Think of it as paying yourself first.

Each pay period, multiply your net income by 10%, which will result in your investment account contribution.

> **TIP:** Once your paycheck hits your checking account, it's a good idea to have your bank account set to automatically send 10% from your checking account to your investment account electronically.

6. **Spend**. When you make it to this step, you can take the vacation you always dreamed of or take your partner to a "pricey" restaurant—you know, like the ones with tablecloths.

(visit www.iamervennelson.com/challenges to share your results.)

# CHALLENGE 3: LET GO OF FEAR

(review lesson 1)

**Comments:**

As the parachute released and we began to descend toward the ground slowly, I was confident that I was safe and had no worries. Since then, I have approached my fears in real life with the same confidence that everything will be all right. Sometimes you think about your ideas or goals too much when all you have to do is jump.

I challenge you to jump on any goal or idea you desired but never fully committed to accomplishing.

**Directions:**

1. Think about why you fear taking a jump on your goal or idea. In the space below, write down these fears in every second line. (This leaves room to write a sentence or two by each fear.)

__________________________________________________

__________________________________________________

__________________________________________________

__________________________________________________

__________________________________________________

__________________________________________________

__________________________________________________

2. Assess what you need to conquer your fears.

3. Before you worry about actions, organize the steps needed to overcome your fears to a timeframe. (Such as a calendar or numbered order.)

4. Now that you know what steps you need to conquer your fears, take action. Commit to executing within your timeframe.

(visit www.iamervennelson.com/challenges to share your results.)

# CHALLENGE 4: SET ATTAINABLE GOALS

(review lesson 2)

**Comments:**

**VALUE System**: Creating efficient goals and the plan to execute them. If you are willing to try this technique, read the insight and information below. You must implement it in your life every day.

**Directions:**

1. **Vision**: Create a mental image of what you want to happen. Once you have a clear picture of your goal, write it down in the "Vision" box below. You must align your vision with your plan. It will encourage you to keep going when you encounter a setback on your journey.

Having a vision will put you 20% closer to accomplishing your goal.

## VISION

2. **Actions**: In the box below labeled "Actions," draw up and execute a plan to reach your desired goal. Be sure to organize timeframes to get stuff done. Don't worry about making it complicated. Just something that you can easily understand.

## ACTIONS

<br><br><br><br><br><br><br><br><br><br><br><br>

Executing the plan above is the key to your success. One way to execute your goal is by breaking it down into smaller, achievable goals. For example, when I clean the kitchen in my house, I divide the area into three sections and work on one task at a time. I start with the dishes, then wipe down the counters and equipment. Lastly, I sweep and mop the floors. This process ensures progress without procrastination.

Decide on a date to update the progress of your goal. You may have to change the deadline or rewrite the plan entirely due to economic reasons or market changes.

Drawing up and executing a plan puts you 40% closer to accomplishing your goal.

**3. Loyalty**: On the lines below, sign your signature to make a firm commitment to the plan you created in the previous step. Your pledge will help you overcome the obstacles on your journey to accomplishing your goal and any other potential resistance to change. By signing on the lines, you are committing to the execution of your plan, no matter what.

_______________________________

_______________________________

Committing to your plan puts you 60% closer to achieving your goal.

4. **Unity**: Identify the team of people you need to collaborate with to get closer to accomplishing your goal. Write their names in the columns below.

| | |
|---|---|
| | |
| | |
| | |
| | |
| | |
| | |
| | |
| | |

Once you have identified the people you need to collaborate with and have established your team, the key is to gain commitment and buy-in to your vision.

Identifying the team of people you need to collaborate with to accomplish your goals puts you 80% closer to achieving your goal.

5. **Evaluate**: In the box below, write your progress towards your goal. (It can be the number of tasks done or what you accomplished up to the date you committed to.) Review your plan and be open to making required changes when they do not happen. This step will provide some accountability and allow you to grow. Be positive during the change process and view change as an opportunity for development.

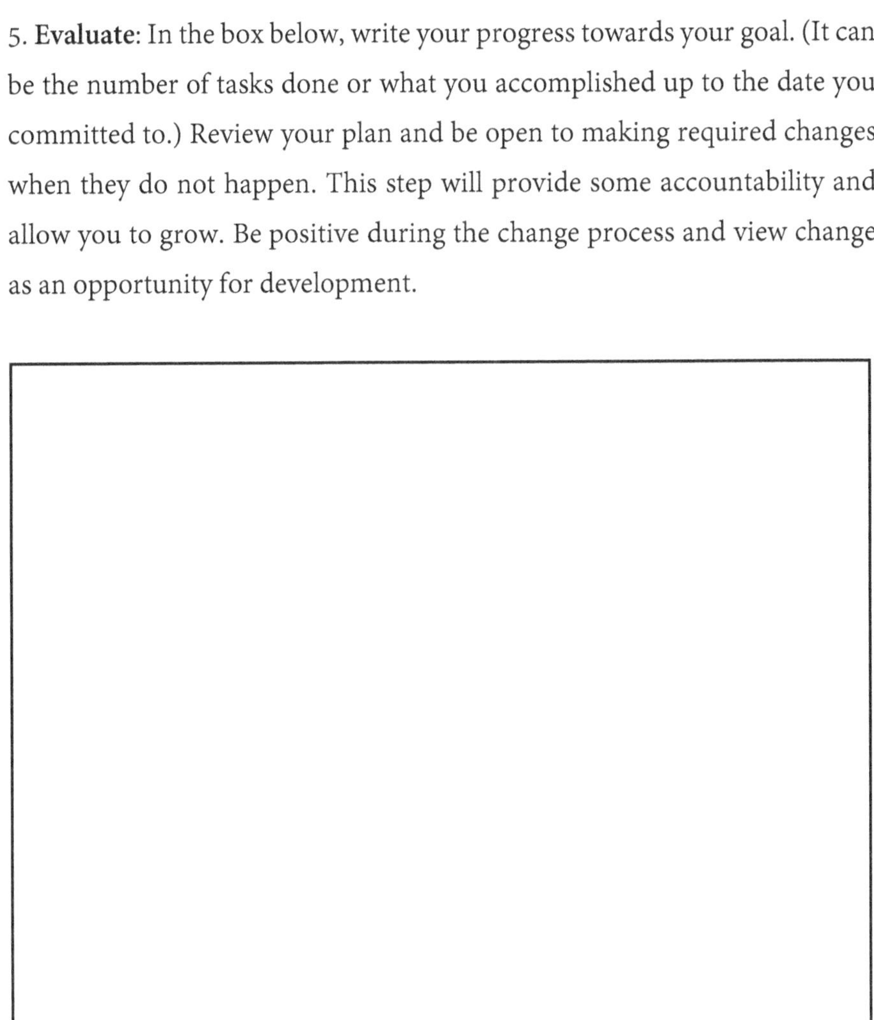

The evaluation period will give you a better understanding of your mistakes and help you consider possible paths for improvement. During this process, consistently communicate results to your team and celebrate the little wins until you complete your goal.

When the goal is complete, you will reach the 100% mark.

(visit www.iamervennelson.com/challenges to share your results.)

# CHALLENGE 5: STRENGTHS & WEAKNESSES

(review lesson 2)

1. In the boxes below, clearly identify your strengths and weaknesses. Strengths are things you can use to push yourself forward. Weaknesses are areas you need to improve on. You must work on your weaknesses and make them as strong as possible while also developing your strengths. Consider bringing someone else on your team whose strengths align with your weaknesses to help you win.

## STRENGTHS

## **WEAKNESSES**

2. Reflect. Reflection enables long-term improvement of all strengths and weaknesses because it gives you a better understanding of yourself and helps you consider a different approach for improvement.

(visit www.iamervennelson.com/challenges to share your results.)

# CHALLENGE 6: FIND YOURSELF

(review lesson 1)

**Comments:**

When you identify what makes your life meaningful, it gives you something to strive for each day. It gives you purpose. This challenge will help reveal who you are meant to be, which will lead to remarkable results.

**Directions:**

1. In the box below, write down what you find meaningful in your life.

2. In the box above, write a series of short sentences that best describe why you find these things important in your life. Be specific.

3. Every time you make a choice, ask yourself, "Is this decision I'm making in line with my vision of myself?"

4. Review this challenge once a week for four weeks. Each week, assess where you are in your life. All the pain, suffering, loss, and failure have contributed to who you are today. Instead of saying, "Life isn't fair," I want you to turn your experiences into motivation and valuable lessons that help you grow.

(visit www.iamervennelson.com/challenges to share your results.)

# CHALLENGE 7: MINIMIZE STRESS

(review lesson 3)

**Comments:**

Stress can lead to health conditions like depression, anxiety, and high blood pressure. I've created The Three P's Method to help you minimize or avoid some of the stress in your life. I have used this method time after time, and it is how I survive overwhelming circumstances. If you are ready to test this technique, read the steps below.

**Directions:**

**Step 1.** Plot. Take deep breaths in and out until you feel released internally. Dwelling on the problem at hand won't make your life any better. It would be best if you had a solution. Identify what caused you to feel stressed, and create a plan for how you will get out of your situation. This step can be incredibly challenging, but I know you can do it.

**Step 2.** Positive Thinking. Challenge yourself to view the perceived stressful circumstance with a positive eye. I want you to think of one experience in your life that made you feel exceptionally grateful. It could be big or small. The purpose of this step is for you to subtitle negative thoughts with gratitude. You created the plan in the first P, so here, in the second P, you are strengthening your mentality, which leads to the third P.

**Step 3.** Perseverance. Stress is temporary, so don't give up too soon because you won't allow yourself to get through it.

(visit www.iamervennelson.com/challenges to share your results.)

# CHALLENGE 8: INVEST IN YOURSELF

(review lesson 5)

**Comments:**

If you discipline yourself, you will notice a difference. It won't be easy to eliminate old habits that usually consume your time, but focus and determination will bring you closer to accomplishing your goal.

**Directions:**

1. In the boxes below, list four trades or skills you possess that have value and potential. Now put them in order by priority. Prioritize what matters to you; what you consider your purpose. In the first box, write down the more important one. For example, if you play an instrument, write down "musician." Conversely, write down "auto mechanic" if you repair or maintain vehicles.

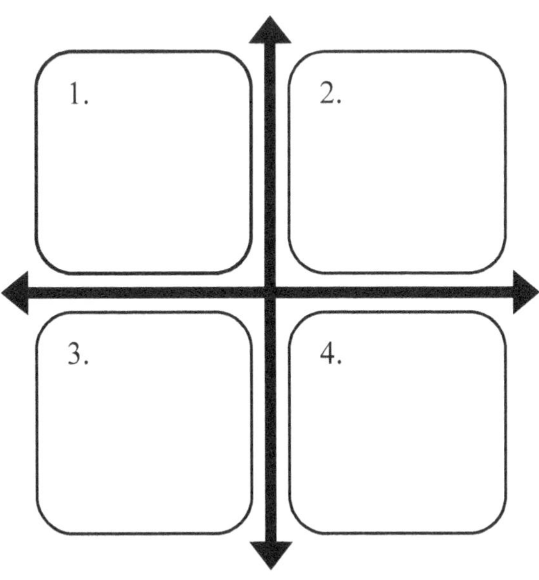

2. For the next 30 days, I want you to read at least one book related to the priority in the first box. If you prefer audio, you could listen to podcasts or YouTube content related to the focus in the first box for a minimum of 30 minutes each day. The goal is to help you organize your goals by priorities and provide you with the habit-building tool you need to help you reach your desired results.

3. After 30 days, re-evaluate. Don't practice every priority at once. After completing this challenge, you can move to the next priority box and repeat the process.

(visit www.iamervennelson.com/challenges to share your results.)

# CHALLENGE 9: RECONDITION YOUR MIND

(review lesson 1)

**Comment:**

Your environment, addictions, and past experiences do not define who you are. Naturally, your mind will adapt to what you put in it. One of the oldest concepts of marketing, the rule of seven, says that a prospective buyer must hear an advertisement at least seven times before being "sold" on a product or service. Today, that number is much higher with social media and the internet. Subconsciously, you are advertising what you want to yourself. The goal is to recondition your mind to define your life how you want it to be.

**Directions:**

1. Choose the words to best describe the goal you want to accomplish. You must speak it into existence. Make sure the words you choose are definite. For example, you could say, "I am a doctor, a lawyer, a musician, a professional athlete, an educator, I will get the promotion at my job," or whatever other goal you desire.

2. Allot seven times throughout a typical day to recite your affirmation. For example, as soon as you wake up and before you go to bed at night. Other examples include when you use the restroom, at meals, when you brush your teeth, and commuting to and from work.

3. After 30 days, re-evaluate. An important note: reconditioning your mind to commit to a goal entirely is not an easy process, and saying the words aloud won't substitute hard work and focus.

(visit www.iamervennelson.com/challenges to share your results.)

# CHALLENGE 10: EVALUATE YOUR NETWORK

(review lesson 6)

1. In the columns below, take inventory of the people you interact with most. Examples of people you interact with are: friends, family, partners, suppliers, supporters, colleagues, vendors, spouses, mentors, and investors.

| NAME | NAME |
| --- | --- |
|  |  |
|  |  |
|  |  |
|  |  |
|  |  |
|  |  |
|  |  |
|  |  |
|  |  |

2. On the columns below, answer the following questions with (Y) for yes or (N) for no:

A) Do they add value to my life?

B) Do they support my ambitions, goals, or dreams?

| NAME | A | B |
|---|---|---|
|  |  |  |
|  |  |  |
|  |  |  |
|  |  |  |
|  |  |  |
|  |  |  |
|  |  |  |
|  |  |  |
|  |  |  |

If you answered no to anyone written in both columns above, consider reducing your footprint with them so you can be at your best for yourself, your loved ones, and your business.

3. After taking inventory of the people you interact with the most and identifying the ones you answered yes to the previous questions, assess your relationship with them. This challenge requires both honesty and deep self-reflection.

One the space below, answer the following questions about the people you answered yes to the previous questions:

1. How can I help fulfill their needs with my skills, trades, time, or other resources?

2. Do I value our relationship?

3. Do I support their ambitions, goals, or dreams?

4. Now, you need to make it right. For example, if you find you're not valuing a relationship enough, ask yourself, "What can I do to reciprocate value to this person?" Write down your thoughts on the space below.

_______________________________________________

_______________________________________________

_______________________________________________

_______________________________________________

_______________________________________________

_______________________________________________

_______________________________________________

_______________________________________________

_______________________________________________

_______________________________________________

_______________________________________________

_______________________________________________

(visit www.iamervennelson.com/challenges to share your results.)

# CHALLENGE 11: PREPARE FOR AN INTERVIEW

(review lesson 6)

**Comments:**

Based on my five years of experience as a hiring manager, here are the top five things recruiters and employers look for in candidates.

**Directions:**

Conduct practice interviews in the same format as the real one. For example, if it's a face to face interview, ask a friend to meet and conduct a mock interview with you to practice answering questions in person. Choose a friend who is willing to give you honest feedback.

### 1. DO NOT Arive Late

❖ Arrive 10 minutes before the interview to anticipate traffic, weather, and loss in direction. It will also give you time to collect your thoughts and mentally prepare.

❖ Early arrival will show employers that you are responsible and possess good time-management skills.

### 2. Let Your Personality Shine

❖ Greet your interviewer with a friendly smile.

❖ Let your personality shine! In some cases, your credentials will not earn you a job opportunity if your personality does not fit their culture and team. Unfortunately, if you and another equally qualified candidate exceeded expectations during an interview, but there is only one position available for the role, the employer will pick the person they liked the most. The key is getting the interviewer to like you as a person just as they want your skills and experience.

## 3. Be Confident

- ❖ Think of an interview as just a conversation between you and the interviewer. Avoid stuttering and long pauses.
- ❖ Maintain eye contact and practice good body language.
- ❖ Try to be relaxed, but use a passionate communication style. One way to build your confidence is to conduct practice interviews in the same format as the real one. For example, if it's a face to face interview, ask a friend to meet and conduct a mock interview with you to practice answering questions in person. Choose a friend who is willing to give you honest feedback.
- ❖ Practice looking in the mirror and answering sample questions out loud.

## 4. Be Prepared

- ❖ Bring extra copies of your resume to the interview.
- ❖ Be ready to share highlights of your career journey for a minimum of five minutes.
- ❖ Prepare 2-3 questions to ask the interviewer.
- ❖ Make sure your clothes are ironed, clean, and presentable.

## 5. Use The SAPL Method

The **SAPL** method is a technique you can use to answer behavioral-based interview questions by discussing the situation, action, positive result of the situation you are describing, and the lesson learned during the process.

- ❖ **Situation**: Describe the situation first.
- ❖ **Actions**: Identify the steps you took to handle the situation.
- ❖ **Positive Result**: What were the results of your actions? Keep it positive. Avoid using a situation with a negative outcome. Talk about some numbers, percentages, or increases you can use when talking about your responsibilities and accomplishments.
- ❖ **Lesson Learned**: Give an example of a lesson you learned that didn't interfere with your ability to get the job done. Did the experience grow your skills?

**SAPL Example:**

Question: Tell me about a time you went above and beyond for a customer.

**Situation:**

One time, at my last retail job, an elderly customer who I had never seen before struggled to carry groceries in one hand while holding a cane in the other for balance and support while walking.

**Actions:**

First, I stopped the tasks I was performing at the time to acknowledge the customer immediately. Then, I asked for her name and offered to free up her hands from the shopping basket she was carrying instead of waiting for her to ask for help. She expressed that she was feeling muscle aches and fatigue but needed to buy a few grocery items for her grandkids visiting on the next calendar day. With her permission, I wrapped her arm around my shoulder to assist her in walking to her vehicle. I gave the customer a pen and paper to write a grocery list and offered to do the shopping for her. I wanted to ensure that someone else was fulfilling my role and adhering to the business needs, so I communicated with other team members over a headset that I would be spending additional time shopping for the customer. Finally, I loaded the groceries into her vehicle and thanked her for choosing to shop at my store instead of local competitors.

**Positive Result:**

The customer completed a survey explaining how she had an exceptional experience, contributing to positive store metrics. The customer is currently a regular customer who visits several times weekly, which is essential to sales and profit growth.

**Lesson Learned:**

The lesson from the scenario was that going the extra mile to make a customer's day leads to business success. Growing sales starts with the experience the customer receives in any business establishment. Since then, I've been striving to make someone's day a little brighter, inside and outside of work.

**5 Sample Questions:**

1. Tell me about a time you went above and beyond for a customer.
2. Tell me about a time you failed. How did you deal with the situation?

3. Tell me about a time when you had to work closely with someone whose personality was very different from yours.

4. Describe a time when your team or company was undergoing some change. How did that impact you, and how did you adapt?

5. Give me an example of a time you managed numerous responsibilities. How did you handle it?

(visit www.iamervennelson.com/challenges to share your results.)

# THE 7 L'S YOU MUST TAKE

To succeed financially and release the "superstar" within

Self-Help & Financial Literacy

ERVEN NELSON

# DISCUSSION QUESTIONS

1. What opportunities have presented themselves to you that you didn't take? Reflect on what held you back. What opportunities have you seized in the past that have been worth it?

2. What two words do you want people to associate with you?

3. Motivation is like drinking a double espresso: it gets you going for a while, but eventually you'll crash. When you feel motivated, suddenly you feel as if you can reach the results you desired instantaneously. How often has a motivational speech gotten you excited about going after your aspirations, only for you to be back to your old habits shortly after? The key is having the discipline to stay motivated and focused until you reach your desired results. What habits are you developing to stay motivated and focused on your desired results?

4. Goals give you direction, and the plan keeps you focused. Describe one short-term attainable goal you set to help you accomplish your long-term goal. Be specific. What progress are you making?

5. Strengths are things you can use to push yourself forward. Weaknesses are areas you need to improve on. What are your strengths and weaknesses? What steps are you taking to improve your weaknesses?

6. When someone asked if I wanted to meet at a pricey restaurant with tablecloths, I would respond with, "I don't have an appetite." Have you ever experienced a similar situation? If so, what are you doing to get back on track with your finances?

7.  What's something you stressed about recently that you realized was perceived as life-threatening and not truly life-threatening?

8.  What skill or trade do you possess with value and potential? How are you investing in yourself?

9.  How are you contributing to society? How does it make you feel?

10. What is the difference between an asset and a liability?

**BONUS QUESTIONS**

11. After reading this book, did you discover something new about yourself that you weren't aware of beforehand? How does it make you feel?

12. What might be your personal experiences related to the reading?

# ABOUT THE AUTHOR

**Erven E. Nelson** is an author and speaker focused on self-help. Despite the struggles of growing up as one of six kids raised by a single mother, he managed to graduate high school and complete two years of technical college. Erven is the founder of the Seven Lessons Foundation, which helps future generations build character and wealth through mentoring and financial empowerment. His integrity, positivity, humility, and passion for excellence have earned him seven promotions in just 8 1/2 years at Wawa, a Fortune 500 corporate retail company. He resides in Florida with a small rescue dog named Ollie. When Erven isn't listening to audiobooks or writing, he is probably composing music or doing a home DIY project.

CONNECT ONLINE

WWW.IAMERVENNELSON.COM